Famous Firsts
in the Ancient Greek
and Roman World

To Betsy, Mike,
and my parents

# Famous Firsts
# in the Ancient Greek
# and Roman World

by David Matz

McFarland & Company, Inc., Publishers
*Jefferson, North Carolina, and London*

ALSO BY DAVID MATZ

*An Ancient Rome Chronology, 264–27 B.C.*
(McFarland, 1997)

*Ancient World Lists and Numbers:*
*Numerical Phrases and Rosters in the Greco-Roman Civilizations*
(McFarland, 1995)

*Greek and Roman Sport: A Dictionary of Athletes*
*and Events from the Eighth Century B.C.*
*to the Third Century A.D.*
(McFarland, 1991)

**Library of Congress Cataloguing-in-Publication Data**

Matz, David.
  Famous firsts in the ancient Greek and Roman world / by David
Matz.
      p.      cm.
  Includes bibliographical references and index.
  ISBN 0-7864-0599-6 (library binding : 50# alkaline paper) ∞
  1. Civilization, Classical — Miscellanea.   I. Title.
DE60.M38   2000
938 — dc21                                              99-52497

British Library Cataloguing-in-Publication data are available

Manufactured in the United States of America

*McFarland & Company, Inc., Publishers*
  *Box 611, Jefferson, North Carolina 28640*
    *www.mcfarlandpub.com*

# Table of Contents

# Introduction

The electronic card catalogue of the University of Pittsburgh's massive system-wide library indicates nearly 4,000 titles containing the word "first." Among them: *Famous First Facts; Firsts: Collecting Modern First Editions; The Firsts of American Jewish History; First Fiction: An Anthology of the First Published Stories by Famous Writers; First Films: Illustrious, Obscure and Embarrassing Movie Debuts; First First Ladies 1789–1865: A Study of the Wives of the Early Presidents; The First Cities; The First Hundred Publications of the Humanities Research Center of the University of Texas at Austin.* Clearly, writers and scholars in a variety of disciplines have seen the value of compiling and publishing catalogues of notable precedents in those disciplines.

This volume on Greek and Roman firsts may also find a place in the literary pantheon of "famous firsts" books and treatises. But perhaps none of these books — nor *any* nonfiction book, for that matter — could justify the paper on which they are printed without answering the famous question first posed by the noted second century B.C. politician and jurist Lucius Cassius Longinus Ravilla: "*Cui bono*?" "Who benefits?"

Who benefits from a book on Greek and Roman firsts? A scholar, professor or teacher may need to know, for example, if the declaration of the *senatus consultum ultimum* directed at the seditious tribune Saturninus was unprecedented. Another scholar might wonder whether the celebrated consular pairing of Pompey and Crassus (who jointly held the consulship in 70 and 55) marked the first time that the same two men held two concurrent consulships, or if there were others. If there were others, who were they? When did they achieve this feat?

A study of the slow but steady climb of the Roman plebeians to a rough equality with the patricians would be enhanced by knowing not only the date and the identity of the first plebeian consul, but of the first plebeians to hold other important positions in the government. A book or a lecture on Greek literature would be more complete if the author or lecturer incorporated information about the first Greek to write about music, or grammar, or civilizations, or botany, or about which Greek first wrote comedies, or geographical treatises, or fables, or critiques of literature.

Who else benefits? Perhaps the high school or college student, who needs information for a term paper or a report, or who simply requires one more bibliographical citation to satisfy the demands of an artificially imposed quota, may find the crucial piece of information here.

The field of classics in general, whose very existence is quite precarious on many contemporary college campuses, also benefits, since its credibility is enhanced, its visibility is increased, by the publication and dissemination of even modest tomes. This is especially true if these books reach, even in small doses, a general readership, which of course comprises another group of beneficiaries. And in the final analysis, this last-named constituency is probably the most important of all.

## *Organization of material*

The material has been organized topically, under the following headings: 1. mythological firsts; 2. firsts in politics, law, and oratory; 3. firsts in military matters and foreign affairs; 4. artistic, architectural and literary firsts; 5. a miscellaneous category, which contains entries that were not logically covered in any of the previous chapters.

Sometimes, an entry would appear to apply to more than one of these categories. For example: *The first book-form reports to the Senate*. When military commanders prepared written reports for the Roman Senate, they customarily wrote them on separate sheets of paper, with no columns or margins. Julius Caesar was reportedly the first commander to make his reports in either scroll or codex form, with columns and margins carefully observed.

The Caesar entry was placed under the category of literary firsts, but it could with equal justification have been slotted in either the military or political sections of the book. In these sorts of situations, where obvious overlap is present, an attempt has been made to place entries in the categories which most readily seem to fit their content.

Likewise, a classification problem emerged when dealing with semi-legendary figures such as Theseus, Odysseus, or Romulus. Should these and others appear in the mythological section, or under the more historically credible categories? The latter option has been employed.

## *Inclusion criteria; sources*

No *termini ante* or *post quem* have been formally observed, but as a practical matter, the book covers Greek and Roman history and civilization from the earliest times, down to the second century A.D. And while the content focuses on Greek and Roman antiquities, occasional information pertaining to other civilizations has also been included, as long as that material was derived from a Greek or Roman source.

An attempt has been made to include the first occurrences of the most significant trends, developments, or milestones in the five categories previously delineated. In such an effort, an author's greater trepidation probably springs more from a fear of sins of omission than of commission; undoubtedly, perspicacious readers will note a few of both. Naturally, the author hopes that these sins will be at a minimum.

That a hierarchy of reliability has long since been established for classical authors cannot be disputed. As a result, when one is seeking information on first century politics, Tacitus is generally preferred to Suetonius; when the Second Punic War is the topic, Livy is considered more accurate and credible than Silius Italicus; the yarnspinning nature of much of Herodotus' *Histories* may appear almost frivolous when compared to the *Peloponnesian War* of the fiercely objective Thucydides. And the works of modern literary critics are sometimes fraught with harshly uncharitable assessments of ancient authors.

This presents a formidable problem for those who accord roughly equal respect to the entire classical corpus. Why should an anecdote from Plutarch or an incident related by the Elder Pliny be discounted simply because it "sounds" improbable, or because it cannot be corroborated by other, allegedly more credible, literary or archaeological sources?

Since this is not the venue for a debate on the relative merits of the classical authors, the discussion will extend no further. However, it must be stated that in this book, material has been derived and presented from the works of a variety of sources, ancient and modern, without prejudice or judgment. Users of this book may, of course, apply their own prejudices if they wish, and choose to accept or reject the value of any specific entry, based on the users' view of the source(s) for that entry. This winnowing, however, is a task best undertaken by the readers, not by the author.

## Bibliographical survey

In writing a book on notable firsts, easily the most useful sources are the many concordances and *indices verborum*, which have been compiled over the years, for many classical authors. A full listing is provided in the bibliography. Suffice it to say that all were of the greatest assistance and value.

Of nearly equal importance are the translations of classical authors which appear in the Loeb Classical Library series. Not only do the renderings usually satisfy that most difficult requirement of the art of translation: "as literal as necessary, as free as possible"; they are also supplemented by informative introductions, learned annotations, and useful indices.

The third edition of the *Oxford Classical Dictionary* is a *sine qua non*. Far more complete in both content and documentation than its two sturdy predecessors, it is a reference resource supremely worthy of a researcher's diligent attention.

The amazingly detailed and superbly annotated *The Magistrates of the Roman Republic*, by T. R. S. Broughton, remains a staple for virtually anyone working on any aspect of that era. Useful mythological resources include J. E. Zimmerman's *Dictionary of Classical Mythology*, Michael Grant's *Myths of the Greeks and Romans*, and Robert Graves' *The Greek Myths*.

From Aeschylus to Xenophon, nearly every ancient author employs in his works forms of the word *protos* or *primus*, often quite generously. So it becomes, then, a matter of degree. Among the Greek authors, Appian was one of the most researcher-friendly in this regard. Other Greek authors who provided much useful and usable material include Diodorus Siculus, Diogenes Laertius, Hesiod, Pindar, Plutarch, and of course, Homer.

Among Roman authors of import should be noted Cicero, Livy, Ovid, Quintilian, Suetonius, and Vergil. Special mention must be made of Gaius Plinius Secundus, Pliny the Elder, the single most important ancient source for the material contained within these pages. While some may take Pliny's monumental *Natural History* with varying amounts of salt (ranging from grains to truckloads), certainly none may deny that Pliny did his homework: 20,000 topics discussed, with information gleaned from 2,000 books written by 100 authors, were all compiled in Pliny's 160 notebooks. Few, if any, ancient authors can match the standard of meticulous documentation which Pliny established. This, in turn, lends at least an aura of credibility to his work that even the most skeptical modern critic must respect.

## Source citations

Ancient authors are cited according to the form of their names most commonly seen, whether anglicized or not. Hence, Pliny (not Plinius, or Gaius Plinius Secundus). If a particular author is noted for one major work only, then the author's name appears without reference to that work, for example: Quintilian 1.3. Authors of multiple works are cited along with titles, for example: Plutarch *Life of Solon* 29.

Translations and other material quoted or derived from the Loeb Classical Library are cited thus: if a single volume, the designation tr. (for "translators"), followed by (LCL) and the page number: tr. Shipley (LCL) 18. If the citation refers to a title in a multi-volume set, the designation tr. will be used, followed by the volume number, (LCL), and the page number: tr. White Vol. III (LCL) 217.

## *Abbreviations employed*

| | | |
|---|---|---|
| CAH | = | *Cambridge Ancient History* |
| CIL | = | *Corpus Inscriptionum Latinarum* |
| DCM | = | *Dictionary of Classical Mythology* |
| LCL | = | *Loeb Classical Library* |
| MRR | = | *Magistrates of the Roman Republic* |
| OCD | = | *Oxford Classical Dictionary* |

## *Dates*

Tradition still exerts a stronger pull on the author than does contemporization. Hence, the designations B.C. and A.D. appear, rather than BCE and CE.

*Category One*
# Mythological Firsts

## Greek Mythology

*Aphrodite's first landing place*

When Aphrodite emerged foam-born from the sea, the first land which she reputedly stepped upon was the island of Cythera (whence her epithet Cytherean). Eventually, she took up residence on Cyprus, the island most often associated with her. (Graves Vol. I 49)

*Apollo's first love*

Apollo's first love was the goddess Daphne. (Ovid *Metamorphoses* 1)

*Athena's inventions*

Athena reputedly invented a number of useful devices, including the flute, the trumpet, the plow, the rake, and the ship (Graves Vol. I 96)

*Cadmus' first cause of grief*

The first bringer of woe to the Theban king Cadmus was his grandson, Actaeon, who aroused the ire of Artemis by inadvertently observing her bathing. Artemis transformed Actaeon into a stag, whereupon he was devoured by his 33 hunting dogs; the first dog to attack was named Melanchaetes. (Ovid *Metamorphoses* 3)

*Daedalus' inventions*

According to Greek mythology, Daedalus was the originator of many devices, including the axe, the wedge, the level, and sails for ships. He designed King Minos' celebrated labyrinth, and also became the first aviator, when he devised mechanical wings for himself and his son, Icarus. (DCM s.v. Daedalus)

### *Deucalion's firsts*

Deucalion was the first man to found cities, construct temples, and rule as a king. (Apollonius of Rhodes 3)

### *The first age of mankind*

Many ancient writers described various ages of mankind; the first was the Golden Age, an epoch of tranquility, happiness, and peace. (DCM s.v. Golden Age). The first adulterers appeared in the *aetas argentea*, Silver Age, or so claims Juvenal (6.24).

### *The first Amazon to confront Hercules*

Hercules' Ninth Labor was to retrieve the girdle of Hippolyta, queen of the Amazons. When he arrived in their territory, he met with firm resistance; a battle ensued. The first Amazon to confront him was Aella. She should have thought better of it: Hercules killed her. (Diodorus Siculus 4.16).

### *The first and only runner to defeat Atalanta*

The swift-footed Atalanta kept intact her vow to remain unmarried by defeating any and all suitors in foot races. The first (and only) suitor to out-run her was Hippomenes (or Melanion, according to some versions of the myth); and he did so only by distracting her by dropping golden apples along the racecourse. (Ovid *Metamorphoses* 10)

### *The first chariot maker*

Erichthonius, the fourth king of Athens, is credited with inventing chariots, and also the harnesses to attach horses to them. (DCM s.v. Erichthonius)

### *The first child eaten by Cronus*

A prophecy given to the Titan Cronus — that he would be overcome by one of his own sons — required desperate countermeasures. So Cronus ate his children, male or female, as they were born. The first child to meet this gruesome fate was Hestia. (Graves Vol. I 39)

### *The first child of Zeus and Metis*

The goddess Athena was the first offspring of Zeus and Metis. Zeus had swallowed Metis when she was pregnant; hence, the noted tale of the birth of Athena from Zeus' head. (Hesiod *Theogony* 895; OCD s.v. Metis)

### *The first child vomited by Cronus*

According to the celebrated myth of Cronus' cannibalistic consumption of his own children, he was eventually compelled to vomit all of them. The first child to be regurgitated was Zeus, possibly because Cronus had ingested in his place an undigestible stone. (Hesiod *Theogony* 497)

### The first dream interpreter

Amphictyon, son of Deucalion and Pyrrha, was credited with two noted firsts: he was the first to interpret dreams and omens, and the first to mix water with wine. (DCM s.v. Amphictyon)

### The first "entity"

Hesiod (*Theogony* 116) asserts that "at the first Chaos came to be" (tr. Evelyn-White [LCL] 87), but he does not specify the nature of Chaos. The term is usually translated as "void," a void soon to be filled by the creation of the next "entity": earth.

### The first finisher claims a bride

The celebrated Libyan strongman Antaeus had only one daughter, but her beauty attracted numerous suitors. Antaeus finally decreed that the suitors must run a race, and that the winner would receive his daughter's hand in marriage. The first man to cross the finish line and thus to claim his new bride was Alexidamus. (Pindar *Pythian* 9)

### The first form of the universe and the first to write about it

The predecessor to the universe was reputedly an amorphous mass, Chaos, from which eventually sprung the gods and human beings. The poet Hesiod was the first to treat these matters in his writings. (DCM s.v. Chaos)

### A first gift to Hercules

The goddess Athena gave Hercules a golden breastplate when he was about to embark upon the first of his Twelve Labors. (Hesiod *Shield of Hercules* 27)

### The first god (Egypt)

Herodotus (2.145) notes that in Greece, Pan is regarded as one of the younger deities, but in Egypt, Pan (or his Egyptian counterpart) is considered to be the first god.

### The first Greek oracle

The earliest Greek oracular shrine was reportedly that at Dodona; it was sacred to Zeus. (OCD s.v. Dodona)

### The first horse races

The god Poseidon was reportedly the originator of horse racing. (Graves Vol. I 60)

*The first kidnapping of Helen*

Although the story of Helen's abduction by Paris is well known, it was not the first time the unfortunate woman had suffered such an outrage. When she was a young girl, Theseus, with the help of his close friend Pirithous, kidnapped her. (Apollodorus *Epitome* 1)

*The first king of Argos*

Inachus, the first king of Argos, reigned 60 years. (DCM s.v. Inachus)

*The first lunar scholar*

The legendary Endymion, with whom the moon goddess Selene fell in love, was regarded by Pliny the Elder (2.43) as the first mortal to observe and study all the facts and facets of the moon. (OCD s.v. Endymion)

*The first mortals to worship the Muses*

The first mortals to worship the Muses were the people of the island of Naxos. (Graves Vol. I 137)

*The first murder trial*

After Ares murdered Halirrhothius, a son of Poseidon, he was tried and found not guilty by a true jury of his peers: the Olympian deities. This was reputedly the first murder trial. (DCM s.v. Alcippe)

*The first musical pipe*

The god Pan is credited with the invention of the pipes, made of wax and reeds. Pan was also reputedly the first to teach the pipemaking trade to humans. (Martial 14.63; Vergil *Eclogues* 2.32)

*The first name in the catalogue of Argonauts*

The first crewman of the Argo named by Apollonius in his catalogue was Orpheus.

*The first of the goddesses*

The oldest, but perhaps least noteworthy, of the offspring of Cronus and Rhea was Hestia — the first Olympian goddess. (Pindar *Nemean* 10)

*The first of 3,000 offspring*

The Titans Oceanus and Tethys produced 3,000 sons. The first of these was Achelous, later venerated as a river deity. (DCM s.v. Achelous)

*The first physicians*

The brothers Podalirus and Machaon — both of whom played important roles in the *Iliad* and in other contexts — were considered in antiquity to be the first mortal physicians. (Celsus *On Medicine: Introduction* 4)

### *The first place visited by Aphrodite after her birth*
Shortly after "foam-born" Aphrodite arose from the sea, she made her way to the island of Cythera, the first place she visited after her miraculous birth. (Hesiod *Theogony* 192)

### *The first prophet*
The first man able to foretell the future was Melampus. He also had the unusual ability to understand the speech of birds and animals, a power granted him when he raised the offspring of two snakes killed by his servants. (DCM s.v. Argos; Morford/Lenardon 353–354)

### *The first questioner to test Tiresias*
Tiresias, the blind prophet, was first put to the test by the nymph Liriope, who asked him if her newly born son Narcissus would live a long life. (Ovid *Metamorphoses* 3)

### *The first race*
The Titans were considered to be the first race. The oldest Titan (and hence, the first) was Oceanus. (DCM s.v. Titans)

### *The first region of the Underworld*
The first region of the Underworld was the Asphodel Fields, where the souls of those who lived lives of neither virtue nor evil reside. (The former were assigned to the Elysian Fields, the latter to Tartarus.) (Graves Vol. I 120–121)

### *The first rulers of Mount Olympus*
Prior to the arrival of Cronus and Rhea, Mount Olympus was under the rule of Ophion and Eurynome. (Apollonius of Rhodes 1)

### *The first sign of the Zodiac*
Aries (the ram) claims the distinction of being the first sign of the Zodiac. (DCM s.v. Aries)

### *The first to attack Thebes*
The first of the Epigoni — the Seven against Thebes — to enter the city was Alcmaeon. (Pindar *Pythian* 8)

### *The first to build an altar for Athena*
The children of the Titan Hyperion were commanded to build Athena's first altar. (Pindar *Olympian* 7)

*The first to help Zeus against the Titans*
When Zeus was in the process of recruiting an army to do battle with the Titans, the first to volunteer was the goddess Styx, oldest daughter of Oceanus. (Hesiod *Theogony* 397)

*The first to think of devious behavior*
Hesiod (*Theogony* 166) asserts that the first deity to engage in deviousness was Ouranos.

*The first to turn on Pentheus*
The Theban king Pentheus surreptitiously viewed a celebration of the Dionysiac rites, off-limits to men. He was subsequently torn to shreds by crazed celebrants when they discovered his presence. Ovid (*Metamorphoses* 3) states that the first woman to see him, and the first to attack, and the first to throw a staff at him, was his own mother, Agave.

*The first use of a winged love charm*
A bird called the iynx (wryneck) was thought to have magical love-inducing qualities. Attaching the bird to a spinning wheel, to create a love charm, was Aphrodite's invention. Jason was the first to utilize the charm, when he used it effectively to evoke Medea's love for him. (Pindar *Pythian* 2; OCD s.v. iynx)

*The first winner in King Minos' funeral games*
When the Cretan ambassador Androgeus was murdered near Athens, King Minos demanded retribution. According to one version of the story, he founded recurrent funeral games in Androgeus' memory, with the prizes to winners being young Athenians. The first winner in these games was Taurus, one of Minos' generals. (Plutarch *Life of Theseus* 16)

*Hercules' First Labor*
Hercules' First Labor was the slaying of the Nemean Lion, a task which he accomplished by strangling the beast. (DCM s.v. Nemean Lion)

*Hercules' first wife*
Hercules' first wife was Megara. When he slew her and their children in a fit of madness, the punishment imposed upon him was the famed Twelve Labors. (DCM s.v. Megara)

*Hermes' firsts and innovations*
The mythographers attribute a number of innovations to Hermes, including:

1. the invention of the lyre
2. the invention of winged sandals
3. the sacrifice of animal offerings to the gods; he was reportedly the first to do this. (DCM s.v. Hermes)

### *Humankind's first encounter with fire*

Prometheus stole fire from the gods and presented it to mortals, their first experience with fire. For this sin, Prometheus was chained to a rock, where his perpetually regenerating liver was incessantly chewed by a vulture. (DCM s.v. Prometheus)

### *Look for Hector's tomb first*

An epitaph recorded by Ausonius:

> Whoever is looking for Priam's tomb should search out Hector's extract first; I first gave that tomb of mine to my son.

### *A minstrel's first and last topic*

A minstrel always praises Apollo first and last in his songs. (*Homeric Hymn* 21)

### *Perdix's innovations*

The sister of the legendary craftsman Daedalus had sent to him her 12-year-old son Perdix to be tutored by his famous uncle. Perdix had already invented the saw blade and the (architect's) compass. Unfortunately, Daedalus' jealousy over his nephew's accomplishments prompted him to throw the youth "from Minerva's citadel"; he later claimed that Perdix had fallen. Minerva, however, caught the plummeting boy in midair, and transformed him into a bird. (Ovid *Metamorphoses* 8; OCD s.v. Daedalus)

### *Pliny's lists of firsts*

Pliny the Elder (7.194–200) records the following firsts in mining, manufacturing, and construction:

| Innovation, profession, commodity | Founder, inventor, first to use | Source |
| --- | --- | --- |
| brick kilns; houses | Euryalus, Hyperbius (Athenian brothers) | not stated |
| clay as construction material | Toxius, son of Uranus | Aulus Gellius |
| first town | Cecrops, founder of Cecropia | not stated |
| first town (alternate source) | Phoroneus, founder of Argos | *aliqui* ("some") |

| Innovation, profession, commodity | Founder, inventor, first to use | Source |
|---|---|---|
| first town (alternate source) | not stated; town: Sicyon | *quidam* ("certain ones") |
| roof tiles; copper mining; tongs; hammers; crowbars; anvils | Cinyra of Cyprus | not stated |
| wells | Danaus | not stated |
| quarrying | Cadmus | not stated |
| walls | Thrason | not stated |
| towers | Cyclopes | Aristotle |
| towers (alternate source) | Tirynthians | Theophrastus |
| cloth | Egyptians | not stated |
| dyed wool | Lydians at Sardis | not stated |
| spindle for wool weaving | Closter, son of Arachne | not stated |
| linen; nets | Arachne | not stated |
| wool production | Nicias of Megara | not stated |
| shoe production; repair | Tychius of Boeotia | not stated |
| medicine | Egyptians | Egyptians |
| medicine (alternate source) | Arabus | *alii* ("others") |
| pharmacology | Chiron | not stated |
| coppersmithing | Lydus of Scythia | Aristotle |
| coppersmithing (alternate source) | Delas of Phrygia | Theophrastus |
| bronzeware production | Chalybes | *alii* |
| bronzeware production (alternate source) | Cyclopes | *alii* |
| ironmaking | Dactyli of Crete | Hesiod |
| silver mining | Erichthonius of Athens | not stated |
| silver mining (alternate source) | Aeacus | *alii* |
| gold mining/production | Cadmus the Phoenician | not stated |
| gold mining/production (alternate source) | Thoas or Aeacus | *alii* |
| medicine produced from minerals | Sun, son of Oceanus | Aulus Gellius |
| tin | (first imported by) Midacritus of Cassiteris | not stated |
| potteries | Coroebus of Athens | not stated |
| potter's wheel | Anacharsis of Scythia | not stated |
| potter's wheel (alternate source) | Hyperbius of Corinth | *alii* |
| carpentry, and various tools, including the saw, axe, plumb line | Daedalus | not stated |
| various tools, including square, lathe, lever | Theodorus of Samos | not stated |
| weights and measures | Phido of Argos | not stated |
| weights and measures (alternate source) | Palamedes | Aulus Gellius |
| fire produced by flint | Pyrodes, son of Cilix | not stated |
| preserving fire in a fennel stalk | Prometheus | not stated |
| four-wheeled vehicle | Phrygians | not stated |
| trade; commerce | Phoenicians | not stated |
| vine and tree growing | Eumolpus of Athens | not stated |

| Innovation, profession, commodity | Founder, inventor, first to use | Source |
|---|---|---|
| wine mixing | Staphylus, son of Silenus | not stated |
| olive oil; olive oil production | Aristaeus of Athens | not stated |
| honey; honey production | Aristaeus of Athens | not stated |
| ox and plow | Buzyges of Athens | not stated |
| ox and plow (alternate source) | Triptolemus | *alii* |
| monarchy | Egyptians | not stated |
| democracy | Athenians | not stated |
| slavery | Spartans | not stated |
| capital trials | Athenians | not stated |

Beginning near the end of Chapter 200, and continuing through Chapter 202, Pliny records the following military innovations:

| | | |
|---|---|---|
| war clubs | Africans | not stated |
| shields | Proteus and Acrisius | not stated |
| shields (alternate source) | Chalcus, son of Athamas | not stated |
| breastplates | Midias of Messene | not stated |
| helmets, swords, spears | Spartans | not stated |
| shinguards, helmet crests | Carians | not stated |
| bows and arrows | Scythes, son of Jupiter | not stated |
| arrows (alternate source) | Perses, son of Perseus | *alii* |
| lances | Aetolians | not stated |
| spears with holsters | Aetolus, son of Mars | not stated |
| light spears, javelins | Tyrrhenus | not stated |
| battle-axes | Penthesilea the Amazon | not stated |
| hunting spears | Pisaeus | not stated |
| catapults | Cretans | not stated |
| slings | Syrophoenicians | not stated |
| bronze trumpets | Pysaeus, son of Tyrrhenus | not stated |
| tortoise screens | Artemo of Clazomenae | not stated |
| rams | Epius | not stated |
| horse riding | Bellerophon | not stated |
| reins and saddles | Pelethronius | not stated |
| fighting on horseback | Centaurs of Mt. Pelion | not stated |
| two-horse chariots | Phrygians | not stated |
| four-horse chariots | Erichthonius | not stated |
| military formations, passwords, sentries | Palamedes | not stated |
| signalling from watchtowers | Sinon | not stated |
| truces | Lycaon | not stated |
| treaties | Theseus | not stated |

Pliny next provides the names of originators and inventors of divination, various musical instruments, singing, dancing, and various kinds of athletic contests:

| | | |
|---|---|---|
| soothsaying from birds | Car | not stated |
| soothsaying from other animals | Orpheus | not stated |

| Innovation, profession, commodity | Founder, inventor, first to use | Source |
|---|---|---|
| soothsaying from sacrificial victims | Delphus | not stated |
| soothsaying from fire | Amphiarus | not stated |
| soothsaying from examining bird entrails | Tiresias of Thebes | not stated |
| dream interpretation | Amphictyon | not stated |
| astronomy | Atlans, son of Libya | not stated |
| astronomy (alternate source) | Egyptians | *alii* |
| astronomy (alternate source) | Assyrians | *alii* |
| globe, especially in astronomical studies | Anaximander of Miletus | not stated |
| origins, nature of winds | Aeolus, son of Hellen | not stated |
| music | Amphion | not stated |
| pipe and flute (single) | Pan, son of Mercury | not stated |
| flute (slanting) | Midas of Phrygia | not stated |
| flute (double) | Marsyas of Phrygia | not stated |
| rhythmical measure (Lydian) | Amphion | not stated |
| rhythmical measure (Dorian) | Thamyras of Thrace | not stated |
| rhythmical measure (Phrygian) | Marsyas of Phrygia | not stated |
| harp | Amphion | not stated |
| harp (alternate source) | Orpheus | *alii* |
| harp (alternate source) | Linus | *alii* |
| seven-string lyre | Terpander | not stated |
| eight-string lyre | Simonides | not stated |
| nine-string lyre | Timotheus | not stated |
| harp without vocal accompaniment | Thamyris (sic) | not stated |
| harp with vocal accompaniment (alternate source) | Linus | not stated |
| songs for harp and singing | Terpander | not stated |
| flute with vocal accompaniment | Ardalus of Troezen | not stated |
| dancing while wearing armor | Curetes | not stated |
| Pyrrhic dance | Pyrrhus | not stated |
| poetic hexameters | Delphic oracle | not stated |
| poetry | uncertain | — — — |
| prose writing | Pherecydes of Syria | not stated |
| history writing | Cadmus of Miletus | not stated |
| gymnastic exercises | Lycaon | not stated |
| funeral games | Acastus | not stated |
| funeral games (at Olympia) | Hercules | not stated |
| wrestling | Pytheus | not stated |
| ball games | Gyges of Lydia | not stated |
| painting | Egyptians | not stated |
| painting in Greece | Euchir | Aristotle |
| painting in Greece (alternate source) | Polygnotus | Theophrastus |

Pliny next provides information about seafaring and shipbuilding firsts:

| Innovation, profession, commodity | Founder, inventor, first to use | Source |
|---|---|---|
| sailing a ship from Egypt to Greece | Danaus | not stated |
| rafts | Erythras | not stated |
| sailing in a long ship | Jason | Philostephanus |
| sailing in a long ship (alternate source) | Parhalus | Hegesias |
| sailing in a long ship (alternate source | Samiramis | Ctesias |
| sailing in a long ship (alternate source) | Aegaeo | Archemachus |
| biremes | Erythraeans | Damastes |
| triremes | Aminocles of Corinth | Thucydides |
| quadriremes | Carthaginians | Aristotle |
| quinqueremes | Salaminians | Mnesigiton |
| ships with six rows of oars | Syracusans | Xenagoras |
| decemremes | Alexander the Great | Mnesigiton |
| ships with up to twelve rows of oars | Ptolemy Soter | Philostephanus |
| ships with up to 15 rows of oars | Demetrius, son of Antigonus | Philostephanus |
| ships with up to 30 rows of oars | Ptolemy Philadelphus | Philostephanus |
| ships with up to 40 rows of oars | Ptolemy Philopator | Philostephanus |
| freighter | Hippus of Tyre | not stated |
| cutter | Cyrenians | not stated |
| boat | Phoenicians | not stated |
| yacht | Rhodians | not stated |
| Cyprian skiff | Cyprians | not stated |
| sailing by the stars | Phoenicians | not stated |
| oar | Copaeans | not stated |
| wide-bladed oar | Plataeans | not stated |
| sails | Icarus | not stated |
| masts | Daedalus | not stated |
| transport ships for cavalry | Samians | not stated |
| transport ships for cavalry (alternate source) | Pericles of Athens | not stated |
| long ships (decked, to accommodate soldiers) | Thasians | not stated |
| beaked bows | Pisaeus, son of Tyrrhenus | not stated |
| anchors | Eupalamus | not stated |
| anchor with two flukes | Anacharsis | not stated |
| grappling hooks | Pericles of Athens | not stated |
| rudder | Tiphys | not stated |
| leading ships in battle | Minos | not stated |

## Priam's first wife and child

The Trojan king Priam was first married to Arisbe; their first child was a son named Aesacus. Priam's first son by his second wife, Hecuba, was the celebrated Trojan warrior Hector. (Apollodorus 3.12)

*A promise to sacrifice the first person*

Idomeneus, the leader of the Cretan contingent at Troy, was beset by a storm at sea en route home after the Trojan War. He promised Poseidon that if he returned home safely, he would sacrifice the first person he saw. Idomeneus survived; unfortunately, upon his arrival he first saw his own son. The ancient authorities differ on the question of whether or not he fulfilled his vow. (DCM s.v. Idomeneus)

*Zeus' first "conquest"*

The first mortal woman with whom Zeus had a sexual relationship was Niobe. Their first child was named Argos. (Diodorus Siculus 4.14)

## Firsts in the Iliad, Odyssey, and Aeneid

### THE ILIAD

*The first battle in the* Iliad *(Book IV)*

The first battle recounted by Homer in the *Iliad* appears in Book IV, a disastrous and bloody engagement in which many warriors on both sides expire. The first man to fall in the battle is the Trojan Echepolus, slain by Archilochus. The first Greek killed in this battle is Leucas, a close friend of Odysseus.

*The first contingent listed in the catalogue of ships (Book II)*

Homer (or perhaps a later cataloguer) provides a lengthy list of the various contingents which comprised the Greek fleet. The first one named is that of the Boeotians, under the joint command of Penelaus, Leitus, Arcesilaus, Prothoenor, and Clonius; they supplied 50 ships.

*The first Greek to die in the Trojan War (Book II)*

Homer identifies Protesilaus, a king of Thessaly, as the first Greek to fall in the Trojan War.

*The first man slain by Achilles (Book XX)*

When the battle resumes with Achilles' full participation, the first Trojan he kills is Iphiton, son of Otrynteus.

*The first named in Zeus' catalogue of conquests (Book XIV)*

When Hera approaches Zeus for lovemaking (and to distract him from the war), he proclaims his desire for her and his amazement at her stunning beauty; none of his paramours, he says, had ever had such an effect on him, not even the first one, the wife of Ixion.

*The first place finishers in the funeral games for Patroclus (Book XXIII)*

In Book XXIII, Homer describes the funeral games sponsored by Achilles in honor of his deceased friend, Patroclus. The first place finishers in the eight contests are as follows:

| Event | Winner |
| --- | --- |
| chariot race | Diomedes |
| boxing | Epeius |
| wrestling | Odysseus and Telemonian Ajax (a draw) |
| foot race | Odysseus |
| sword fight | Diomedes |
| discus throw | Polypoites |
| archery | Meriones |
| javelin throw | Meriones (by default) |

*The first to address Achilles (Book IX)*

The Greeks send an embassy to the sulking Achilles, to urge him to return to the fighting. The first member of the entourage to address Achilles is Odysseus; his appeal is unsuccessful.

*The first to breach the Greek wall (Book XII)*

The Trojan attack on the Greek wall is led by Sarpedon, who is the first to create a gap in it; he does this with his bare hands. The first Trojan to fall in the assault is Epicles, Sarpedon's friend. The killer: Ajax, son of Telamon.

*The first to break the truce (Book IV)*

The truce between the Greeks and the Trojans (arranged so that Paris and Menelaus could engage in one-on-one combat) is broken by the Trojan warrior Pandarus, who shoots an arrow at Menelaus and wounds him.

*The first to engage Hector (Book VI)*

Hector challenges any of the Greeks to step forward to meet him in single combat. Since no Greek volunteers, a lottery system is implemented, with Ajax, son of Telamon, thus chosen. The long confrontation between the two is inconclusive.

*The first to kill an enemy (Book XIV)*

After the battle described in this book concludes, Homer catalogues some of the warriors who survived, and others who did not. The first to kill an enemy soldier: Ajax, son of Telamon, who vanquished Hyrtius.

*The first to oppose Agamemnon's proposal to flee (Book IX)*

At the outset of Book IX, Agamemnon appears before the assembled

Greeks, and suggests that they return to Greece, since it is becoming apparent that they will not win the war. The first to respond to this proposal is Diomedes, who angrily rejects it.

### The first to see the return of Hector's body (Book XXIV)

When Priam and Hermes return to Troy with the body of Hector, the first to observe them is Cassandra.

### The first to volunteer for a night mission (Book X)

In Book X, Homer describes a night raid carried out by the Greeks against the Trojans. Although several men discuss the planning of the raid (including Nestor, both Ajaxes, Archilochus, Agamemnon, and Menelaus), Diomedes is the first to volunteer to participate. He chooses Odysseus as his co-conspirator. The first man whom they kill on their mission is Dolon, who, ironically, was on *his* way to gather reconnaissance about the deployment of the Greek forces; Dolon had been the first (and only) Trojan to volunteer.

### The first words of the Iliad and the Odyssey

In both the *Iliad* and the *Odyssey*, Homer attempted to convey significant themes by his choice of a first word in each epic.

In the *Iliad*, the first word (in Greek) is *menin*, which means "anger," referring specifically to the anger of Achilles; his often ungovernable anger dictates many of his actions in the *Iliad*, and since he is a key figure in the epic, his anger becomes a central theme.

In the *Odyssey*, on the other hand, the first Greek word is *andra*, meaning "man," and referring to Odysseus. This indicates that the thoughts and actions of Odysseus will play central roles in the story.

### Odysseus and Diomedes in the front row (Book XIX)

When Achilles summons an assembly of the Greeks to announce his intention to reconcile with Agamemnon and rejoin the war, Odysseus and Diomedes occupy the front seats.

### Two Patroclean firsts (Book XVI)

After Patroclus dons Achilles' armor, he rallies his fellow soldiers to drive the Trojans away from the Greek ships. In this battle, Patroclus is the first to throw a spear, and the first to hit an enemy soldier, Pyrechmes.

## ——— THE ODYSSEY ———

### Athena's first shape shift (Book I)

Athena assumes many forms and disguises in the *Odyssey*. The first of these occurs early in Book I, when she appears in Ithaca as the Taphian commander Mentes.

*The first characters Odysseus meets on Ithaca (Books XIII, XIV)*

Odysseus finally brings to a conclusion his ten-year voyage home when he lands on the shores of Ithaca (or more accurately, is placed there by the Phaeacians). The first character whom he sees is Athena, disguised as a herdsman. The first human whom he encounters is Eumaeus, his now elderly swineherd.

*The first ones to recognize Odysseus (Books XVI, XIX)*

When Odysseus returns to Ithaca, he arrives disguised as a beggar. The first one to whom he reveals his true identity is his son, Telemachus. However, the first person to recognize him without the benefit of his assistance is Eurycleia, his childhood nurse. She is about to wash his feet when she notices on his thigh a scar from a boyhood hunting accident. She remembers the incident, and instantly knows that the beggar is indeed Odysseus.

*The first Phaeacian athlete to challenge Odysseus (Book VIII)*

The hospitable Phaeacians invite Odysseus to observe their athletic contests. Eventually, one of their number, Euryalus, arrogantly challenges Odysseus to compete. Odysseus, in anger, picks up a discus and hurls it farther than any of the Phaeacian throwers.

*The first Phaeacian king (Book VI)*

According to Homer, the first Phaeacian king, Nausithoos, settled his people on the island of Scheria, where he constructed temples and homes, and also assigned lands to farmers.

*The first place visited by Odysseus after the Trojan War (Book IX)*

Odysseus' ten-year journey following the Trojan War carried him to many bizarre and fantastic locales; the first of these was Ismarus, the land of the Cicones, where Odysseus and his men kill many of the inhabitants, and plunder their possessions.

*The first place visited by Telemachus (Book III)*

Odysseus' son Telemachus embarks upon a journey to attempt to glean information about his long-lost father. The first place which he visits on this quest is Pylos, home of Nestor, oldest and wisest of the Greeks who fought at Troy.

*The first shade seen by Odysseus in the Underworld (Book XI)*

When Odysseus makes his voyage to the Underworld, the first shade which he sees is that of Elpenor, one of his former comrades; he died when he tumbled off the roof of Circe's palace.

### The first suitor to die (Book XXII)

When Odysseus begins slaying the suitors who had shamelessly pursued his wife in his absence, the first one whom he shoots is Antinoos, the most obnoxious of all 108 suitors.

### The first suitor to try the bow (Book XXI)

When Penelope announces to the suitors that she will marry the one who can string and shoot Odysseus' bow, the first to attempt the feat is Leodes, a soothsayer. He — like all the rest — fails in the effort.

Before all others, however, Odysseus' son Telemachus tries, with no success.

### The first to string the bow (Book XXI)

In the famous test of the bow, Odysseus is the first (and only) man able to string it; the suitors for Penelope's hand in marriage had failed to do so.

### Odysseus' debut (Book V)

Although Homer focuses upon the man — Odysseus — in the *Odyssey*, Odysseus himself does not appear in the story for the first time until the fifth book.

## —— THE AENEID ——

### Aeneas' first wife (Book II)

Aeneas' first wife, Creusa, fails to survive the fall of Troy. When Aeneas returns to search for her, she appears to him as a ghost, instructing him to leave, and telling him his destiny lies elsewhere.

### The first Greek seen by Aeneas (Book II)

On the fateful night when the Greeks are ransacking Troy (immediately after the success of the Wooden Horse), Aeneas briefly tries to rally his Trojan friends in opposition. The first Greek whom they encounter — Androgeus — they kill.

### The first landfall in Italy (Book VI)

When Aeneas and his followers finally arrive in Italy, the first town they enter is Cumae.

### The first man out of the horse (Book II)

According to Vergil, nine Greeks are concealed within the hollow body of the Wooden Horse. The first one (named in Vergil's catalogue) to slither out of the horse in the dead of night is Sthenelus.

### The first place to which Aeneas flees after the fall of Troy (Book II)
Aeneas and a small band of friends and family (including his son Ascanius and his aged father Anchises) first flee to Mount Ida after the sack of Troy. The first place they reach after having set sail is Thrace, where they first attempt to settle and found a new city.

### The first sign of battle (Book IX)
As the Trojan and Latin armies advance against one another, a javelin flying through the air is the first indication that battle is imminent. The first to rally the Trojans to fight is the warrior Caicus.

### The first skirmish between Trojans and Latins (Book VII)
The first skirmish between the Trojans and Latins erupts when Ascanius kills a deer, which unfortunately happens to be a pet of Tyrrhus, herdsman of King Latinus. The Latins attempt to ambush Ascanius for the deed, only to be stymied by Trojan intervention.

### The first to civilize Latium (Book VIII)
The god Saturn was the first deity to be associated with Latium; he is credited with collecting together the wild inhabitants of the mountains and providing them with laws. He also reputedly coined the place name Latium.

### The first to join the Latins (Book VII)
The Etruscan king Mezentius, along with his son Lausus, are the first Italians to join forces with Turnus and his Latins, in opposition to Aeneas.

### The first to set fire to the ships (Book V)
In an effort to prevent the Trojans from leaving Sicily, Juno directs Iris to appear to the Trojan women, and exhort them to burn the ships. Iris, disguised as the matronly Trojan woman Beroe, is the first to hurl a burning torch into the midst of the vessels. The first Trojan woman to see through Iris' disguise is the old nurse, Pyrgo.

### The first Trojan War incident described by Aeneas (Book II)
When Aeneas begins his long account of the Trojan War for the Carthaginian queen Dido, the first incident which he describes is the trick by which the Greeks won the war: the Wooden Horse.

*The man who first came from the shores of Troy (Book I)*

The word *primus* appears in the *Aeneid*'s first line, the sixth word in the epic; it refers to Aeneas as the first man to escape the burning walls of Troy.

*Underworld firsts (Book VI)*

When Aeneas journeys to the Underworld, the first shades he sees are those of infants; later, he sees Dido. When he ultimately makes his way to the Elysian Fields (dwelling place of those whose lives had been virtuous), the first soul whom he encounters is that of his father, Anchises.

*Winners in the funeral games for Anchises (Book V)*

To honor his deceased father Anchises, Aeneas organizes a series of athletic competitions. The contests, and those who took first place, are as follows:

| Contest | Winner |
| --- | --- |
| boat race | Cloanthus (the captain) |
| foot race | Euryalus |
| boxing | Entellus |
| archery | Acestes |

The games concluded with the running of the first-ever Troy game, featuring young men on horseback doing various coordinated maneuvers and tricks. Aeneas' son Julus (Ascanius) instituted the Troy game in Alba Longa, where it was transmitted from one generation to the next, down to historical Roman times.

## Roman Mythology

*The first (and possibly only) devotio*

A *devotio* was a ritualized prayer in which the petitioner sought the help of the gods in defeating his enemies and "devoting" them to the Underworld. The only well documented use of the *devotio* occurred in 340 B.C., during Publius Decius Mus' preparations for battle against the Latins. (Livy 8.9; OCD s.v. *devotio*)

*The first god named in prayer*

As the Roman god of beginnings, Janus was customarily named first in prayers. Examples can be found in Livy (8.9) and Martial (8.8; 10.28).

*The first god to wear a wreath*

Pliny the Elder (16.9) suggests that the god Bacchus was the first to wear a leaf crown, in his case one composed of ivy.

*Priam's original name*

The first name applied to King Priam of Troy was Podarces. (OCD s.v. Priam)

*Three firsts of Ceres*

According to Ovid (*Metamorphoses* 5; *Fasti* 4), Ceres was the first to cultivate fields, provide the lands with crops, and give laws.

*Category Two*

# Firsts in Politics, Oratory, Law, Government

## *Greek*

*Alcibiades' first assembly appearance*

Alcibiades happened to be passing an Assembly meeting one day when he heard a sudden cheering and applause. When he inquired about the reason for the uproar, he was told that an *epidosis* (voluntary series of donations to the state) was underway. Alcibiades approached the speaker's platform to announce a largesse of his own, his first official act in an Assembly meeting.

As a sort of sidebar to the incident, Plutarch (*Life of Alcibiades* 10) notes that a quail which Alcibiades had concealed beneath his cloak escaped shortly after his presentation, causing a considerable distraction to the Assembly attendees.

*Alcibiades' first place of exile*

After Alcibiades left with the Athenian fleet for Sicily (415 B.C.), an impeachment was passed against him, regarding his alleged participation in the sacrilege of the Eleusinian Mysteries. When he learned of the indictment, he fled from the fleet, first landing at Thurii, in southern Italy. Shortly thereafter, he defected to Sparta. (Plutarch *Life of Alcibiades* 22–23)

*The ancient world's first superpower*

According to Velleius Paterculus (1.6), the Assyrians (circa 2200 B.C.) were the first race to attain preeminence in world affairs. They were succeeded in turn by the Medes, the Persians, the Macedonians, and finally, the Romans.

*Antiphon's firsts*

Antiphon was the first Greek known to employ the so-called periodic style in his writings. He was also the first ghostwriter of speeches. (OCD s.v. Antiphon; CAH V 24)

*Athens' first major demagogue*

Prior to the mid–fifth century B.C., Athenian statesmen had sprung from the ranks of established, sophisticated families. The first politician of note to rise to power from humbler origins was the demagogue Cleon, Pericles' great rival, and the butt of many an Aristophanic joke.

Cleon's first known verbal assaults on Pericles occurred in 431 and 430. (CAH IV 106–107; OCD s.v. Cleon)

*Cleisthenes' innovations*

In the late sixth century B.C., the Athenian politician Cleisthenes introduced a number of governmental/political innovations, including:

1. The virtual replacement of the traditional four Athenian tribes with ten new ones, based on geographical, rather than socio-economic, considerations.
2. The establishment of the Council of 500, consisting of 50 representatives from each of the ten tribes, whose primary responsibility was to set the agenda for the Assembly.
3. The creation of the ten-year period of exile system known as ostracism.

Cleisthenes apparently attempted to implement a system of government based upon the notion of *isonomia* ("equal rights," or "law"), thus serving as the foundation for the flowering of the Athenian democracy in the following century. (OCD s.v. Cleisthenes [2])

*Demosthenes' first attempt at public speaking*

The greatest Greek orator of all, Demosthenes, hardly enjoyed an auspicious debut. His first speech in public was so disorganized and so poorly delivered that his audience broke out in laughter. He persevered, however, and through various drills and exercises was able to dramatically improve his speaking voice and his physical presence. (Plutarch *Life of Demosthenes* 7)

*Difficulties with the prima littera*

According to Cicero (*On the Orator* 1.260), Demosthenes initially experienced so much difficulty in speaking without stuttering that he could not pronounce the *prima littera*, "first letter" (r), in the very profession in which he desired to excel: rhetoric.

*The earliest extant works of an Attic orator*

The orator Antiphon (circa 480–411 B.C.) is thought to have been the first to compose and commit to writing speeches for courtroom plaintiffs. Hence, they are the oldest extant speeches. (OCD s.v. Antiphon [1])

*The first apolitical ostracism victim*

When ostracism votes were established in 488 B.C., the first victims were politicians who were thought to have tyrannical sympathies. The first ostracized Athenian not known for these leanings was a certain Xanthippus. He was ostracized around 485, for simply being "too great," i.e. apparently overbearing in egotism or self-pride. (Aristotle *Athenian Constitution* 22.6)

*The first archon*

The first Athenian archon was Medon, son of the last king, Codrus; the traditional date of his office was 1068 B.C. Medon and his successors held the office for life, until 753 B.C., when Charops became the first archon to be limited to a term of ten years. Beginning in 683, the office became an annual magistracy; the first one-year archon was Creon. (Velleius Paterculus 1.2, 8; Shipley [LCL] 6, 18)

*The first assessment on Delian League members*

The Delian League — a confederacy of Greek city-states, with Athens at its head — was formed in 478 B.C. In 477, the first dues assessment was imposed upon league members; it amounted to 460 talents, payable to Athens as the league member primarily responsible for the protection of the others. (Thucydides 1.96; CAH IV 44)

*The first Athenian to judge Pisistratus correctly*

Although he was aiming at a tyranny, Pisistratus had a dissimulative way of speaking which helped to conceal his true objectives. Solon, however, was the first Athenian to see through the glib veneer and to discern Pisistratus' plans. (Plutarch *Life of Solon* 29)

*The first codification of law*

The first Greek law code was composed by the Locrian lawgiver Zaleucas around 650 B.C. He was the precursor of the Athenian Draco, and his legislation was equally severe. (Cicero *Letters to Atticus* 6.1; OCD s.v. Zaleucas)

*The first demagogue*

According to Plutarch (*Life of Theseus* 32), Menestheus, a great grandson of Erechtheus, was the first man to engage in demagoguery, thus hoping to gain influence over the masses.

### The first demagogue elected general

A sheep dealer named Lysicles rose to political power shortly after the death of Pericles in 429 B.C.; he eventually became the first demagogue elected general (in 428), sharing the post with Nicias. Plutarch (*Life of Pericles* 24, quoting Aeschines) states that Lysicles owed his lofty position to his marriage with the politically well-connected courtesan Aspasia. (Scott-Kilvert 190)

### The first ephor

When the ephors (Spartan political leaders) were established, the first holders of the designation were Elatus and his associates. (Plutarch *Life of Lycurgus* 7)

### The first florid elocutionist

Eratosthenes reputedly claimed that the philosopher Bion was the first "to deck philosophy with bright-flowered robes," a reference to his propensity for using a multitude of oratorical styles in his speeches. (Diogenes Laertius 4.52; tr. Hicks [LCL] 431)

### The first funeral speech

During times of war, it was customary in Athens for a leading citizen to deliver an annual public eulogy for soldiers who had died in battle in the previous year. The first Athenian known to have delivered such a speech (*epitaphios*) was Pericles, in 440 B.C. during a war with Samos. (OCD s.v. *epitaphios*)

### The first histrionic orator

According to Plutarch (*Life of Nicias* 8), the demagogue Cleon was the first Athenian orator to incorporate into his speeches various attention-getting devices: shouting; terms of abuse; thigh-slapping; perambulating along the speaker's platform as he harangued the audience.

### The first known use of the graphe paranomon

The *graphe paranomon* was a decree passed to obviate an action of the Assembly or the Council of 500, which (action) was deemed unconstitutional or illegal. The first known use of this device occurred in 411 B.C., during the Revolution of the 400. (OCD s.v. *graphe paranomon*)

### The first ostracism victim

The first man to fall victim to an ostracism vote was Hipparchus, of the deme of Cholargus; he was related to the tyrant Pisistratus. The date was 488 B.C. (Plutarch *Life of Nicias* 11)

### The first president of the Hellenotamiai

The Hellenotamiai were Athenian officials whose duty was chiefly to manage the finances of the Delian League. When the playwright Sophocles served as one of these officials (443–442 B.C.), he was listed as the leading member, perhaps the president. This marked the first time that anyone was honored in this way. (Lesky 273)

### The first requirements of an orator

Before all other qualities, an orator must possess these two: self-confidence, and a stentorian voice. (Dionysius of Halicarnassus *Isocrates* 1)

### The first Sicilian tyrant

The first Sicilian tyrant was Panaetius, ruler of Leontini, in the sixth century B.C. (OCD s.v. Leontini)

### The first stipend for Assembly attendance

The meetings of the Athenian Assembly (open to all citizens) were often relatively poorly attended. So sometime in the fourth century B.C., the Athenian politician Agyrrhius introduced a measure whereby attendees would be rewarded with the payment of one obol; the stipend was later increased to two and ultimately to three obols. (OCD s.v. Agyrrhius)

### The first stipend for attendance at plays

Sometime in the fourth century B.C., Athenian citizens first began receiving stipends from the state to facilitate their attendance at plays. The politician who introduced this practice is thought to have been Eubulus, although some sources indicate that Agyrrhius (the same man who instituted payments for attending Assembly meetings) was the promulgator. (OCD s.vv. Eubulus; theorika)

### The first time archons were chosen by lot

The nine archons, who shared supreme power in Athens, were elected by the citizenry until 487 B.C., when a lottery system was used for the first time. This greatly reduced their influence in the government. (OCD s.v. archontes)

### The first to bribe a jury

Anytus (one of the three prosecutors of Socrates) had led a fleet of 30 triremes to Pylos in 409 B.C., attempting to expel the Spartans then occupying it. However, he failed to accomplish his mission and, upon returning to Athens, was put on trial. He gained acquittal by bribing the jurors, the first Athenian defendant ever to engage in bribery. (Aristotle *Athenian Constitution* 27.5; Rackham [LCL] 83)

### The first to compile oratorical rules

Antiphon was the first orator to compile and disseminate a compendium of rhetorical *technai*, the foundations of the art of oratory. Some authorities also consider him to have been the first to ghostwrite speeches for litigants in lawsuits. (Plutarch *Moralia* 832C, E)

### The first to devise a mixed constitution

Lycurgus of Sparta was the first Greek lawgiver to devise a constitution containing elements of kingship, aristocracy, and democracy. (Polybius 6.3)

### The first to differentiate between contentious and political speeches

The first orator to differentiate between "contentious speeches and those of a political character" was Isocrates; he specialized in the latter genre. (Plutarch *Moralia* 837 B; tr. [LCL] Fowler 373)

### The first to emphasize politics in the study of oratory

According to Dionysius of Halicarnassus (*Isocrates* 1), the orator Isocrates was the first to emphasize politics and political science in the study of oratory, thus providing incipient orators with the skills and knowledge necessary to serve the government most effectively.

### The first to employ metaphorical expressions

Dionysius of Halicarnassus (*Lysias* 3) relates that Gorgias of Leontini was the first orator to attract the attention of Athenian audiences with the use of metaphors.

### The first to employ schemata

Isaeus was reputedly the first orator "to give artistic form [*schematizein*] to his speech." (Plutarch *Moralia* 839 F; tr. [LCL] Fowler 389)

### The first to use concise language

Dionysius of Halicarnassus (*Lysias* 6) considered Lysias to have been the first orator to use concisely worded arguments.

### The first to use prose rhythms

According to Cicero (*Brutus* 32–33), the first orator to use and teach rhythm and measured diction was the Greek Isocrates.

### The first tyrant

The first ruler to be called a tyrant was the Lydian king Gyges, who reigned from approximately 685 to 657 B.C. Coins were also minted for the first time in the ancient world during Gyges' tyranny. (OCD s.v. Gyges)

### The first welfare payments to Athenian citizens

The late fifth century B.C. Athenian politician Cleophon initiated a system of daily, two-obol stipends (*diobelia*) to citizens who (it is thought) were not otherwise receiving government subsidies. (OCD s.v. Cleophon)

### The first western Greek colony

The island of Pithecusae (near Naples) was the first Greek colony in the west, founded in the eighth century B.C. (to be distinguished from the first *mainland* colony, Cumae). (OCD s.v. Pithecusae)

### Solon's first stop on a ten-year journey

After Solon had reformed Athens' laws (594 B.C.), he decided to take a ten-year voyage. The first place he visited was Egypt, where he studied philosophy, and also learned of the legend of Atlantis. (Plutarch *Life of Solon* 26)

### Themistocles' first place of exile

A few years after the Battle of Salamis (480 B.C.), Themistocles' consistently arrogant behavior caused the Athenians to ostracize him. He lived in many places during his exile; the first was Argos. (Plutarch *Life of Themistocles* 23)

## Roman

### Alternate first consuls

According to an alternate version of the story, the first two consuls were not Brutus and Poplicola, but Brutus and Lucius Tarquinius Collatinus. This version states that Tarquinius resigned soon after taking office, with Poplicola replacing him. (MRR Vol. I 2)

### Augustus' first thought of restoring the republic

Once Augustus had seized power in Rome, only twice did he consider the possibility of restoring the republic. The first time was in 30 B.C., directly after the Battle of Actium. (Suetonius *Life of Augustus* 26)

### Caesar in first place

When it became clear to all that Julius Caesar was a force to be reckoned with in Roman politics, he used to assert that it would be more difficult for his enemies to demote him from the first rank (*primus ordo*) to the second, than it would be to degrade him from the second to the last. (Suetonius *Life of Julius Caesar* 29)

### Caesar's first act as praetor

Upon assuming the praetorship in 62 B.C., Julius Caesar's first act was the interrogation of Quintus Lutatius Catulus regarding the lack of progress in various renovations to the capitol, under Catulus' direction. (Suetonius *Life of Julius Caesar* 15)

### Caesar's first military campaign

In 81 B.C., Julius Caesar went to Asia to serve on the staff of the provincial governor there, Marcus Thermus. In the following year, he was sent to Mitylene, where he was given the civic crown (awarded for saving the life of a fellow soldier in battle). These events represented his first taste of military duty. (Suetonius *Life of Julius Caesar* 2)

### Caesar's first political office

In 70 B.C., Julius Caesar entered into the office of military tribune, the first elective office which he held. (Suetonius *Life of Julius Caesar* 5)

### Catiline's first foray into politics

According to Cicero (*Handbook of Electioneering* 9), Catiline's *primus ad rem publicam aditus*—"first appearance in political affairs"—was marred by the execution of several Roman knights by Gallic nationals whom Catiline was supposed to have been supervising.

### Cicero's first case

Cicero's first criminal case, and one of the first (of any classification) which he argued was the *Pro Roscio Amerino (In Defense of [Sextus] Roscius of Ameria)*, in 80 B.C. It was also the first speech to which Plutarch referred in his biography of Cicero. Roscius had been accused of parricide; Cicero won an acquittal. (Freese *Cicero: Pro Quinctio* [etc.] [LCL] 112)

### Cicero's first consular task

According to Plutarch (*Life of Cicero* 12), Cicero's first major policy task as consul in 63 B.C. was to assuage the nobility's fears that pending legislation about land distributions and the raising of new troops would harm their interests. He accomplished this primarily by speaking out against the legislation, thereby effecting its defeat.

### Cicero's first perception of the decline of Roman law courts

When Cicero testified against Publius Clodius Pulcher in 61 B.C., at the latter's trial for sacrilege, and Clodius won an acquittal from a bribed jury, it marked the first time in Cicero's long public career that he began to doubt the integrity and the incorruptibility of Roman law courts. (Cowell 191)

### Ciceronian consular firsts

Cicero was not only the first member of his family to attain the consulship;

he was also the first "new man" (*novus homo*) to be elected to the consulship in his first year of eligibility for the post. Cicero's first act as consul, on his very first day in office (January 1, 63 B.C.) was to denounce an agrarian reform measure proposed by the tribune Publius Servilius Rullus. (Cicero *On the Agrarian Law* 2.3; Freese *Cicero* Vol. VI [LCL] 335)

### Ciceronian oratorical firsts

According to Tacitus (*Dialogue on Oratory* 22), Cicero was the first to bestow upon oratory its mature, polished form, and also the first to use vocabulary and syntax in a logical, effective, and sophisticated manner.

### Cyprus' first quaestor

In a short letter to Sextilius Rufus, Cicero (*Letters to Friends* 13.48) encourages Rufus on the latter's assuming office as the first quaestor in Cyprus.

### The first Catilinarian conspirator to be executed

Five men were eventually convicted for their roles in Catiline's conspiracy. Ultimately, all five were executed; the first to suffer this punishment was Publius Cornelius Lentulus Sura. (Plutarch *Life of Cicero* 22)

### The first century to vote

Rome's electoral assembly, the Comitia Centuriata, consisted of 193 voting units or blocks, "centuries." The first century to vote in an election (the *centuria praerogativa*, randomly chosen and always composed of patricians) could significantly sway the results of an election, since its votes were tallied and announced before members of any of the other centuries marked their ballots. Because many Romans believed that candidates favored by the *centuria praerogativa* were also favored by the gods, their reluctance to offend the celestial powers often influenced their own votes.

Elections of individual officeholders displayed the same auspicious advantages of priority: there were multiple holders of all the major governmental offices, and therefore multiple electoral winners. But the winning candidates whose names were announced first were regarded more favorably and accorded more respect than those who followed, even if all the winners were equally well qualified. (Cicero *Pro Murena* 18; MacDonald *Cicero* Vol. X [LCL] 206, 563)

### The first choice to succeed Hadrian

The emperor Hadrian's first choice to succeed him in office was Lucius Aelius Caesar. However, Aelius died before Hadrian's wishes could be fulfilled. (OCD s.v. Aelius Caesar, Lucius)

### The first colony outside Italy

The first Roman colony outside Italy was founded on the site of ancient

Carthage, as a part of Gaius Sempronius Gracchus' legislative program. The date was 122 B.C. (Velleius Paterculus 2.7)

### The first consul with a non–Latin nomen

Marcus Perperna was the first consul (130 B.C.) with a non–Latin family name; "Perperna" was of Etruscan origin. (OCD s.v. Perperna [1])

### The first consuls to assume office on January 1

Prior to 153 B.C., the Roman calendar year began on March 1. When the changeover to January 1 took place, the first two consuls to assume office on the new starting date were Quintus Fulvius Nobilior and Titus Annius Luscus. (MRR Vol. I 452)

### The first consuls with two quaestors apiece

According to Dio (48.43), the consuls Appius Claudius and Gaius Norbanus (38 B.C.) "were the first to have two quaestors apiece as associates." Dio also notes that in this year, no fewer than 67 men held the office of praetor, apparently in quick succession!

### A first-day resignation from the consulship

Mark Antony, chosen as one of the consuls for 34 B.C., resigned on his first day in office; Dio (49.39) gives no reason. He was replaced by Lucius Sempronius Atratinus, who subsequently resigned on July 1. His successor: Paullus Aemilius Lepidus.

### The first day after an evil emperor

In A.D. 70, the satirist Curtius Montanus castigated the orator Marcus Aquilius Regulus; in the course of his speech, he asserted that "the best day after [the demise of] an evil emperor is the first day." (Tacitus *Histories* 4.42; OCD s.v. Curtius Montanus)

### The first desideratum in court cases

According to Cicero, in any court case, no matter how important or how trivial the offense, the first point which needs to be established and proved is motive. (*In Defense of Sextus Roscius* 62)

### The first dual dictators

The office of dictator was almost always a sole magistracy, but on rare occasions, two dictators were appointed. This occurred for the first time in 217 B.C., when a second dictator, Marcus Minucius Rufus, was chosen to occupy the post concurrently with Quintus Fabius Maximus. The same situation occurred in the following year, after the disastrous Battle of Cannae, when Marcus Junius Pera and Marcus Fabius Buteo served as dictators. (Plutarch *Life of Fabius Maximus* 9)

### The first election of military tribunes

Military tribunes had traditionally been chosen by dictators or consuls. In 311 B.C., the right of selection of (16) military tribunes was granted to the voters; they were also given the right to elect two naval commanders annually. These measures were enacted at the behest of Lucius Atilius, Gaius Marcius and Marcus Decius, all tribunes of the people. (Livy 9.30; MRR Vol. I 161)

This seems to have been the first year in which such elections were systematized; however, Livy (7.5) also refers to elections of military tribunes as early as 362.

### The first eloquent Roman orator

According to Cicero (*Brutus* 57), the first Roman to whom documented eloquence could be attributed was the second century orator Marcus Cornelius Cethegus. Cicero quotes Ennius' laudatory description of Cethegus: *Suaviloquens os*, "smooth-speaking mouth."

### The first emperor to hold the office of consul suffect

The emperor Claudius held four consulships during this reign (in A.D. 42, 43, 47, 51). He was consul suffect in 47, the first time that an emperor had ever held that kind of consulship. (Suetonius *Life of Claudius* 14)

### The first exhibition of a camelopard

A bizarre beast called a camelopard was exhibited in Rome for the first time in 46 B.C., by Julius Caesar. This animal resembled a camel, except for its leopard-like spots (Dio 43.23)

### The first exile in his own country

During the chaotic times following the publication of the proscription list in 43 B.C., many of the proscribed attempted to flee, some implementing ingenious plans for escape. A certain Sittius, a leading citizen of Cales (near Naples), was one of those unfortunates whose name appeared on the list. His fellow townsmen, however, interceded on his behalf so effectively that the triumvirs agreed to let him live, as long as he did not leave Cales — thus making Sittius the first (and possibly only) man to be an exile in his own country. (Appian *Civil Wars* 4.47)

### The first foreign-born consul

When Spanish-born Lucius Cornelius Balbus gained the consulship in

40 B.C., he became the first consul not born on Italian soil. (OCD s.v. Balbus [3])

### The first Gallic-born consul

Publius Alfenus Varus, suffect consul in 39 B.C., was the first Gallic-born holder of that office. He was also a legal scholar, and compiled a systematic compendium of statutes and laws; he was the first to apply the term *Digesta* (*Digest*) to such a compilation. (OCD s.v. Alfenus Varus, Publius)

### The first governor of Egypt

The first Roman governor of Egypt was Gaius Cornelius Gallus. His mal-administration of the province led to his eventual recall, and ultimately to his suicide in 26 B.C. (OCD s.v. Cornelius Gallus, Gaius)

### The first impeachment

In 133 B.C. the efforts of the tribune Tiberius Sempronius Gracchus to implement land reforms were frequently scuttled by the intercession of a rival tribune, Marcus Octavius. The exasperated Gracchus eventually asked the tribal assembly to move forward with an impeachment vote on Octavius, the first such instance of a deposition of a legally elected Roman official. (Boren 96)

### The first inexpensive grain

The plebeian aedile Manius Marcius was the first government official to provide inexpensive grain for sale. The price: one *as* per peck; the date: 456 B.C. (Pliny the Elder 18.15)

### The first instance of a parricide conviction and punishment

A particularly cruel method of execution was imposed upon defendants convicted of parricide: to be sewn into a cloth sack along with a dog, a chicken, a monkey, and a snake, with the entire assemblage hurled into a lake or river. The first known victim was the matricide Publicius Malleolus, in 102 B.C. (although the practice apparently began during the monarchy). (Cicero *In Defense of Sextus Roscius* 69–70; Livy *Epitome* 68; Schlesinger *Livy* Vol. XIV [LCL] 82)

### The first irregularly chosen princeps senatus

The princeps senatus was traditionally expected to have first held the office of censor. However, in 209 B.C., the censors charged with the selection of a princeps senatus disagreed on the appropriate candidate. One censor, Marcus Cornelius Cethegus, insisted on following the traditional method of selection, whereas the other censor, Publius Sempronius Tuditanus, favored offering the post to Quintus Fabius Maximus, the *princeps Romanae civitatis,* "first man of the Roman state." Tuditanus prevailed, and Fabius Maximus was named to the post. (Livy 27.11; MRR Vol. I 285)

### *The first juridicus*
In imperial times, a policy evolved of appointing judges (*juridici*) to preside over court cases in Italy (i.e., outside of Rome). The first known *juridicus* was selected by Marcus Aurelius, in A.D. 163. (OCD s.v. *juridicus*)

### *The first king of Cyrene*
The first king of the African city of Cyrene was Battus, mentioned by Catullus in poem number seven.

### *The first land distributions*
Livy (31.3) asserts that the first effort to provide land distributions to veteran soldiers occurred in 201 B.C., at the conclusion of the Second Punic War. Lands in Samnium and Apulia were earmarked for this purpose, and a commission of ten men was appointed to administer the process. The ten appointees: Publius Servilius, Quintus Caecilius Metellus, Gaius Servilius Geminus, Marcus Servilius Geminus, Lucius Hostilius Cato, Aulus Hostilius Cato, Publius Villius Tappulus, Marcus Fulvius Flaccus, Publius Aelius Paetus, and Titus Quinctius Flamininus.

### *The first law dealing with extortion*
During his tribunate (149 B.C.), Lucius Capurnius Piso was the first to propose and carry a law concerning extortion. (Cicero *Brutus* 106; OCD s.v. Piso [1])

### *The first law specifying age restrictions for office holders*
The first *lex annalis* was passed in 180 B.C.; it specified minimum ages for holders of curule magistracies, including 42 for the consulship. The law's chief proponent was the tribune Lucius Villius. (OCD s.v. Villius)

### *The first legions to support Vespasian*
When Vespasian began his push toward the emperorship in A.D. 69, the first legions to declare their support for him were those in Egypt, under the command of the prefect Tiberius Alexander. (Suetonius *Life of Vespasian* 6)

### *The first limitations on courtroom oratory*
Pompey the Great was the first to impose certain restrictions on courtroom oratory. In particular, prior to his time, pleaders could speak for hours

on end. Pompey made some effort to require speakers to conclude their remarks in a reasonable period of time. (Tacitus *Dialogue on Oratory* 38)

### The first magister equitum to appoint a city prefect

Mark Antony became the first magister equitum to appoint a *praefectus urbi* (city prefect) when he tapped his uncle, Lucius Julius Caesar, for the post in 48 B.C. (Dio 42.30)

### The first man slain in the proscriptions

The first man slain in the proscriptions of 43 B.C. was a tribune by the name of Salvius. When he learned that his name had been placed on the list, he organized a sumptuous banquet for himself and his friends, realizing that it would probably be his last opportunity to do so. He was prescient; soldiers broke into the midst of the festivities, attacked and decapitated Salvius, and commanded the horrified banqueters to remain where they were, or they, too, would be executed. (Appian *Civil Wars* 4.17)

### The first man to hold seven consulships

Gaius Marius was the first man in Roman history to hold the consulship seven times. The previous record-holder, Marcus Valerius Maximus Corvus, was a six-time consul (348, 346, 343, 335, 300, 299 B.C.). Marius was also the first politician to hold the office as many as five years consecutively (104–100; his other two terms were in 107 and 86). (Plutarch *Life of Marius* 45; OCD s.v. Marius)

### The first man to lose two elections in one day

When Gaius Marius ran for the office of curule aedile (circa 118 B.C.), it became clear early in the day's voting that he would be defeated. So he hastily withdrew from that race, and instead offered his candidacy for the plebeian aedileship. The result, however, was the same, thus making Marius the first Roman politician to lose two elections on the same day. (Plutarch *Life of Marius* 5)

### The first military tribunes with consular powers

Military tribunes with consular powers assumed their magistracies for the first time in 444 B.C.; the office was created in response to plebeian-patrician friction. The first three such tribunes: Aulus Sempronius Atratinus; Lucius Atilius Luscus; Titus Cloelius (Dionysius of Halicarnassus 11.61; Livy 4.7). According to Foster's annotation of Livy ([LCL Vol. IV] 277), military tribunes and consuls continued to be chosen until 367, when the former office was abolished. During the period 444–367, "consuls were chosen twenty-two times and tribunes fifty-one times."

*The first name on the proscription list (43 B.C.)*

When the triumvirs (Augustus, Mark Antony, Lepidus) drew up a list of men slated for execution, Mark Antony refused to cooperate in the process unless Cicero's name appeared first on the list. Lepidus sided with Antony; Augustus, after some initial hesitation, also assented to Antony's wishes. (Plutarch *Life of Cicero* 46) Other sources suggest that the first man so "honored" was Lucius Aemilius Paullus, who escaped execution and eventually made his way to Asia. (OCD s.v. Aemilius Paullus [3])

*The first non-senatorial imperial legal adviser*

The highly regarded lawyer Masurius Sabinus (fl. first century A.D.) became a legal adviser to the emperor Tiberius, the first non-senator to be elevated to a post of such distinction. (OCD s.v. Masurius Sabinus)

*The first of the tyrannicides to be killed*

Of the conspirators who participated in the assassination of Julius Caesar, the first one to suffer a similar fate was Gaius Trebonius. Trebonius was asleep in his bed in Smyrna when soldiers loyal to Publius Cornelius Dolabella burst into the room. Trebonius offered to accompany them for an interview with Dolabella, when one replied: "Go where you please, but you must leave your head behind here, for we are ordered to bring your head, not yourself." (Appian *Civil Wars* 3.26; tr. White Vol. II [LCL] 567)

*The first orator to address the people directly*

It had long been customary for Roman orators to face the Senate house when speaking in the forum, thus (symbolically, at least) addressing the Senate, to the exclusion of the general populace. Gaius Sempronius Gracchus was the first orator to abandon this practice; his speaking orientation always faced the citizenry. (Plutarch *Life of Gaius Gracchus* 5)

*The first Pater Patriae*

According to Plutarch (*Life of Cicero* 23), Cicero was apparently the first Roman to be granted the honorary title *Pater Patriae*, "Father of the Country." He received the sobriquet through the efforts of Marcus Porcius Cato, for his (Cicero's) actions in suppressing the Catilinarian conspiracy.

*The first patrician to transfer to plebeian rank*

The most prominent Roman patrician to obtain a *traductio ad Plebem*— transfer to plebeian rank (to gain eligibility for the tribunate) — was undoubtedly Publius Clodius, in 58 B.C.

Clodius, however, was not the first; that distinction belongs to Decimus Junius Silanus, who was adopted into the plebeian family of Titus Manlius Torquatus in 140 B.C. (Schlesinger *Livy* Vol. XIV [LCL] 48–49)

*The first permanent criminal court*

Rome's first permanent criminal court — the *quaestio de rebus repetundis* (for trying cases of provincial mismanagement) — was established in 149 B.C. The tribune Lucius Calpurnius Piso was instrumental in its creation. (MacDonald *Cicero* Vol. X [LCL] 416)

*The first plebeian curule aedile*

A certain Juventius was reportedly the first plebeian elected curule aedile. The date: 306 B.C. (Cicero *Pro Plancio* 58; MRR Vol. I 166)

*The first plebeian dictator (also the first plebeian censor)*

Gaius Marcius Rutilus claims two noted firsts: he was the first plebeian dictator, in 356 B.C., and five years later, in 351, he became the first plebeian to hold the censorship. His successful defense of Rome against an Etruscan invasion resulted in the first Roman presence in Ostia (later to become Rome's port city).

Rutilus was also a four-time consul (in 357, 352, 344, and 342). (Livy 7.17.6; 7.22.6–10; OCD s.v. Marcius [2])

*The first plebeian maximus curio*

The 30 *curiae* were each supervised by an official called the *maximus curio*, a post traditionally held by patricians. However, in 209 B.C. — after a period of political maneuvering — the first plebeian gained the office: Gaius Mamilius Atellus. (Livy 27.8; MRR Vol. I 289)

*The first plebeian praetor*

The first plebeian to hold the office of praetor was Quintus Publilius Philo, in 336 B.C. He also held four consulships, in 339, 327, 320, and 315. (Livy 8.15; MRR Vol. I 139) See also *The political firsts of Quintus Publilius Philo.*

*The first plebeian priests and augurs*

Priesthoods were the last important offices to be made available to plebeian candidates (who had gained eligibility to the other major magistracies in 367 B.C.). So in 300 (or possibly 296), the tribunician brothers Quintus and Gnaeus Ogulnius proposed and passed a law raising the number of augurs from five to nine, and pontiffs from four to eight, with the number of plebeians set at four and five, respectively. The first four plebeian pontiffs: Publius Decius Mus; Publius Sempronius Sophus; Gaius Marcius Rutilus; Marcus Livius Denter. The first five plebeian augurs: Gaius Genucius; Publius Aelius Paetus; Marcus Minucius Faesus; Gaius Marcius Rutilus; Titus Publilius. (Livy 10.9; MRR Vol. I 172–173)

### The first pontifex maximus elected in absentia

According to Velleius Paterculus (2.3), the high esteem in which Publius Cornelius Scipio Nasica Serapio was held enabled him to be the first man elected pontifex maximus *in absentia*; the year was 141 B.C. (MRR Vol. I 478)

### The first pontifex maximus who held no prior offices

When Publius Cornelius Calussa was elected pontifex maximus in 332 B.C., it marked the first time that any Roman politician had held the office without occupying any prior elective office. The feat was not duplicated for another 120 years, when Publius Licinius Crassus was elected pontifex maximus under similar circumstances. (Livy 25.4; MRR Vol. I 142)

### The first priest convicted in a criminal court

The augur Gaius Sulpicius Galba (fl. late second century B.C.; held office in 109) claimed the dubious distinction of being the first Roman priest to be convicted in a criminal court. The charge: conspiratorial behavior during the war with Jugurtha. (Cicero *Brutus* 127; OCD s.v. Sulpicius Galba [1])

### The first proposal for agrarian reform

Although the Gracchan brothers are perhaps the most noted land reform proponents in Roman history, they were not the first to promote such proposals. According to Livy (2.41), the first politician to propose allotting lands to plebeians was Spurius Cassius, in 485 B.C. Cassius met a fate similar to that of Tiberius and Gaius Gracchus: execution.

### The first proscriber

When the Second Triumvirate published its proscription list in 43 B.C., Marcus Aemilius Lepidus was listed as its first author and implementer, followed by Mark Antony and Augustus. Lepidus and Antony both proscribed relatives (Lepidus his brother Paullus, and Antony his uncle Lucius Caesar), principally because Paullus and Caesar had been the first to vote Lepidus and Antony enemies of the state. (Appian *Civil Wars* 4.12)

### The first public sacrifices for an individual's health

When Pompey fell ill in early 49 B.C. while leading his army to Campania, many cities in Italy vowed public sacrifices to hasten his return to health, and for his safety. This marked the first time that any Roman leader was so honored. (Dio 41.6)

### The first published legal proceedings

The *legis actiones*—"legal actions"—were first published and disseminated to the public by Gnaeus Flavius, around 305 B.C. Prior to this time, all such information was held in confidence by the pontiffs and other select citizens.

Pliny the Elder asserts that it was about at this time that rings came into vogue as fashion statements. (Pliny the Elder 33.17, 20; OCD s.v. Flavius, Gnaeus)

### The first requirement for an orator

A prospective orator must first of all be a *vir bonus*, "good man," i.e., one of unimpeachable integrity. (Quintilian [Preface] 1.9)

### The first Roman police chief

The emperor Augustus established the ancient Roman equivalent of a police force, the *cohortes urbanae*, urban cohorts. The first leader (*praefectus*) of the force was Marcus Valerius Messalla Corvinus, around 26 B.C. However, Valerius resigned after only a few days, claiming that he did not possess the expertise needed to manage the office. (Tacitus *Annals* 6.11; OCD s.vv. *cohortes urbanae*; Valerius Messalla Corvinus, M.) See also *The first urban prefect (II)*.

### The first Roman province in Asia

When the Romans annexed Pergamum in 133 B.C. it attained the distinction of becoming Rome's first Asian province. (Boren 64)

### The first Roman visited by Parthian ambassadors

When Parthian ambassadors paid a visit to Lucius Cornelius Sulla, it marked the first time that they had ever met with a Roman statesman in an official capacity. According to Velleius Paterculus (2.24), several soothsayers in the delegation predicted that Sulla's life and reputation would be godlike.

### The first salaried rhetoric teacher

When Quintilian (circa A.D. 35–100) received a salary drawn from the public treasury, it marked the first time that any Roman teacher of rhetoric was compensated in this way; the emperor Vespasian initiated the payments. (OCD s.v. Quintilian)

### The first seating regulation

Marcus Roscius Otho, in his praetorship in 67 B.C., was the first to propose a law which reserved the first 14 rows of seats in theaters and amphitheaters for equestrians. (Plutarch *Life of Cicero* 13) However, some scholars believe that Otho's legislation merely reaffirmed earlier seating regulations.

### The first signs of oratorical decline

In his *Dialogue on Oratory* (28), Tacitus assigns to one of the speakers

(Messalla) the statement that the decline of oratorical eloquence and related endeavors first began in Rome, spread throughout Italy, and from there, overseas.

### The first slave freed by the vindicta

During the consulship of Lucius Junius Brutus (509 B.C.), a conspiracy to restore the monarchy arose. It was quelled in part because of information given to Brutus by a slave named Vindicius. This Vindicius was hence granted his freedom by the *vindicta* (referring to the ceremonial touching with a staff); Vindicius was the first slave to be freed by this process. (Livy 2.5)

### The first smooth speaking Latin orator

Cicero believed that the second century B.C. orator Marcus Aemilius Lepidus Porcina was the first to display a "smoothness of diction and periodic sentence form." (Cicero *Brutus* 95–96; Rose 100; tr. Hendrickson [LCL] 87)

### The first teenaged consul

When Augustus usurped the consulship at the age of 19 in 43 B.C., it marked the first time that anyone so young had occupied the office. (Suetonius *Life of Augustus* 26)

### The first to agitate for citizenship for the Italians

The first prominent politician to lobby on behalf of native Italians in their quest for Roman citizenship was Marcus Fulvius Flaccus; he used this as a campaign issue en route to his election to the consulship for 125 B.C. (Appian *Civil Wars* 1.34; OCD s.v. Fulvius Flaccus [1])

### The first to assail Mark Antony

In the months following Julius Caesar's death, the political community seemed somewhat cowed by Mark Antony. Cicero, of course, attacked him in the *Philippics*; however, the first politician to publicly castigate Antony in the months after the Ides of March was Lucius Calpurnius Piso, the slain Caesar's father-in-law. (Cicero *Letters to Friends* 12.2; Williams Vol. II [LCL] 522)

### The first to inform against Catiline

A certain Quintus Curius allegedly was the first to approach the Roman Senate with details about Catiline's conspiracy of 63 B.C. For his services, the Senate voted him an unspecified sum of money. (Suetonius *Life of Julius Caesar* 17)

### The first to join Galba

When Servius Sulpicius Galba gained the emperorship in A.D. 68, his first important supporter was his eventual successor, Marcus Salvius Otho. (Tacitus *Histories* 1.13)

### The first to praise Caesar's murderers

Lucius Cornelius Cinna, praetor in the fateful year of 44 B.C., was the first politician of note to publicly praise Caesar's assassins and their deed. The result: some of Cinna's audience was made up of Caesar's loyal veterans, men who did not take kindly to hearing their leader's murder legitimatized. So they threw rocks at Cinna, chased him from the speaker's platform, and nearly burned down the house to which he fled. This, says Appian, was the first public manifestation of support for the slain dictator. (Appian *Civil Wars* 1.121)

### The first to publish information about legal proceedings

Legal procedures, and especially court calendars, were not accessible to the general populace in Rome's early history. However, in 304 B.C., a curule aedile of lowly birth named Gnaeus Flavius reputedly obtained and published this information, the first time it had been disseminated to the public. (Cicero *Letters to Atticus* 6.1; *Pro Murena* 25; Livy 9.46)

### The first to ratify imperial favors

The emperor Tiberius and all subsequent emperors refused to acknowledge favors granted to individuals by previous emperors unless they themselves confirmed these favors on a case by case basis. The emperor Titus was the first to break with this tradition, by issuing a blanket decree endorsing all previously granted favors. (Suetonius *Life of Titus* 8)

### The first to receive consular powers without having been a consul

When Publius Cornelius Scipio Africanus was awarded consular powers in 210 B.C., it marked the first time that any Roman politician or military leader had received such a distinction without first having held the consulship. (OCD s.v. Cornelius Scipio Africanus [the elder], Publius)

### The first to resign full dictatorial powers

According to Appian (*Civil Wars* 1.3), Lucius Cornelius Sulla was the first man to voluntarily surrender the sort of all-encompassing powers bestowed by a first century B.C. dictatorship, and to offer to expose himself to an accounting by any citizen who might wish to do so.

### The first to speak after Caesar's assassination

Mark Antony delivered his famous eulogy on Julius Caesar shortly after the dictator's murder in 44 B.C. He was the first official to speak publicly on the matter. (Plutarch *Life of Cicero* 42)

*The first to speak against the Catilinarian conspirators*

In the Senate's debate over the fate of the Catilinarian conspirators (December 63 B.C.), the first speaker was Decimus Junius Silanus, consul-elect for 62. He recommended imprisonment and the "supreme penalty," which most in the audience understood to mean execution. The first (and only) senator to oppose the death penalty was Julius Caesar. The first to speak against Caesar's proposal (for imprisonment of the conspirators) was Quintus Lutatius Catulus, consul in 78 and a longtime opponent of Caesar's. (Appian *Civil Wars* 2.5; Plutarch *Life of Cicero* 21)

*The first to stab Caesar*

As the famous Ides of March plot against Julius Caesar unfolded, the first man to stab him was Publius Servilius Casca (Suetonius *Life of Julius Caesar* 82)

*The first to stab Pompey*

When Pompey fled to Egypt after the Battle of Pharsalus (48 B.C.), he rode ashore in a small boat, accompanied by several of King Ptolemy XIII's servants. Pompey thought that he recognized one of these as a Roman soldier he once knew. When the boat landed, he asked the soldier, named Sempronius (or Septimus in some accounts), whether they had ever met. The soldier nodded; but as Pompey turned to leave, Sempronius stabbed him, with the others following suit. (Appian *Civil Wars* 2.85)

*The first to utilize oratorical propriety*

Cicero (*Brutus* 82) states that the second century B.C. orator Servius Sulpicius Galba was the first to perform *oratorum propria et ... legitima opera*, "appropriate and legitimate tasks of orators": well-placed digressions; sensitivity to the audience; sufficient explication of the matter at hand.

*The first to worship Caligula as a god*

The "divine" Caligula's claim to that exalted epithet was confirmed by the first person of note to worship him as such: the future emperor Vitellius. (Suetonius *Life of Vitellius* 2)

*The first trial for poisoning*

In 331 B.C., a deadly pestilence afflicted Rome, or so it seemed. However, a servant woman approached one of the aediles, Quintus Fabius Maximus, with information that several conspiratorial women had been poisoning the city's food and water supplies. When Fabius Maximus and the consuls confronted several of these women in the act of preparing their concoctions, the women claimed that the potions which they were producing were health-enhancing drugs. The informer challenged them to consume the potions; after some hesitation, they did so, and died.

Eventually, 170 Roman matrons were tried for the crime of poisoning, the first such trial in the city's history. Livy does not relate the outcome of the trial, nor the women's motives, but he does state that they were judged to be demented, an early instance of the insanity defense. (Livy 8.18)

### The first tribunes

The first tribunes of the people took office in 493 B.C. Livy (2.33) implies that the Senate chose two, Gaius Licinius and Lucius Albinus. These two then selected three others as their colleagues; Livy provides one name: Sicinius. Dionysius of Halicarnassus (6.89) gives these five names: Lucius Junius Brutus; Gaius Sicinius Bellutus; Gaius and Publius Licinius; Gaius Visellius Ruga.

In 471, tribunes were elected for the first time by the tribal assembly. The first five so elected: Gnaeus Siccius, Lucius Numitorius, Marcus Duillius, Spurius Icilius, Lucius Maecilius. A few years later, in 457, the plebeians agitated for an increase in the number of tribunes, from five to ten; they obtained this concession, in exchange for their acquiescence to the patrician demand that no tribune could stand for re-election. (Livy 2.58 and 3.30; MRR Vol. I 41)

### The first two consuls to twice occupy the office as colleagues

The first two politicians to hold the consulship twice as colleagues were Aulus Sempronius Atratinus and Marcus Minucius Augurinus, in 497 and 491 B.C. Other pairs: Lucius Papirius Cursor and Spurius Carvilius (293 and 272); Quintus Aurelius Cotta and Publius Servilius Geminus (252 and 247); Quintus Fabius Maximus Verrucosus and Tiberius Sempronius Gracchus (215 and 213, although Fabius Maximus was a suffect in 215).

The only colleagues who held the office two years in a row were Lucius Cornelius Cinna and Gnaeus Papirius Carbo in 85 and 84.

Perhaps the most famous consular pair was Marcus Licinius Crassus and Gnaeus Pompeius Magnus (Pompey the Great), in 70 and 55. (MRR Vol. I 12, 212)

### The first two plebeian censors

The year 131 B.C. marked the first time that two plebeians occupied the office of censor: Quintus Caecilius Metellus Macedonicus and Quintus Pompeius. Metellus delivered a celebrated speech in this year, in which he proposed that marriage be required by law.

Another first in 131: a consul who concurrently held the office of pontifex maximus. This dual office-holder was Publius Licinius Crassus. (Livy *Epitome* 59; MRR Vol. I 500)

*The first two plebeian consuls*

The first election of two plebeians to the consulship occurred in 173 B.C. The winners: Gaius Popilius Laenas and Publius Aelius Ligus. (Livy 42.9)

*The first unlimited dictatorship*

Roman dictators were supposed to remain in office a maximum of six months. The first man to exceed this time limit, and thus to create a virtually unlimited dictatorship, was Lucius Cornelius Sulla (dictator from 82 or 81 to 79 B.C.) (Appian *Civil Wars* 1.99)

*The first urban prefect (I)*

In Rome's earliest days, an urban prefect was selected to govern the city when the king, or later the consuls, was absent. The first holder of the office was reputedly Denter Romulius, an appointee of Romulus. (Tacitus *Annals* 6.11)

*The first urban prefect (II)*

The need for an urban prefect diminished with the creation of praetors, who assumed the responsibilities of that office. Later, however, the post was reinstated and reformed under Augustus; its holder was, in effect, a chief of police. Augustus' first appointee, Messalla Corvinus, whose tenure lasted only a few days, departed the office after discovering that he had no competence in administering it. (Tacitus *Annals* 6.11; OCD s.v. praefectus urbi)

*The first use of the fasces to represent political authority*

According to Juvenal (8.268), the fasces came to symbolize the authority of magistrates during the reign of Servius Tullius.

*The first use of the senatus consultum ultimum*

The *senatus consultum ultimum*, "final decree of the Senate," a form of martial law, was first used in 121 B.C., to deal with the violence spawned by the reform proposals of Gaius Sempronius Gracchus. The *s.c.u.* was applied under similar circumstances ten more times in the following 80 years. The final declaration of an *s.c.u.* occurred in 40 B.C., at the instigation of Augustus, against Salvidienus Rufus, a onetime associate of Augustus, who later deserted to Mark Antony's cause. (OCD s.vv. Salvidienus Rufus; *senatus consultum ultimum*)

*The first variation in the price of salt*

Salt had been customarily sold at the same price throughout Italy. But in 204 B.C., one of the censors, Marcus Livius, imposed a price on salt higher for outlying towns than for Rome. According to Livy (29.37), he did this because he was still bitter over a perceived injustice he had suffered in a court case, a situation for which he blamed these townsmen. Hence, the increase in their costs for this valuable commodity. Livy adds that Livius acquired the cognomen Salinator ("salt dealer") as a result of this incident.

### The first virtue in speaking

Avoiding faults is the *prima virtus*, "first virtue" in oratory. Some of these faults include: foul language; inappropriate choice of words; monotonous delivery; the mixing of colloquial expressions with sophisticated words and phrases. (Quintilian 8.3)

The first virtue in eloquence, according to Quintilian (2.3), is clarity.

### The first woman displayed at a triumph

In one of Julius Caesar's triumphal processions in 46 B.C.— he had five — he displayed among his captives Arsinoe, Cleopatra's sister. This was the first time that a woman of royal birth had been paraded before the Roman people in a triumph, and many of them thought it improper. (Dio 43.19)

### The firsts — and seconds — of Servius Sulpicius Rufus

Cicero's close friend, the noted jurist Servius Sulpicius Rufus, studied the art and science of oratory in Rhodes. Cicero states that Servius returned to Rome preferring *in secunda arte primus esse ... quam in prima secunda*, "to be first in the second skill [science of oratory] rather than second in the first skill [art of oratory]." Cicero also asserts that his friend enjoyed the first rank of all those who had studied or practiced civil law. (Cicero *Brutus* 151)

### The founder of the cui bono principle

The *cui bono* principle — "to whose benefit?" as a criterion for determining motive in a criminal proceeding — was first articulated by Lucius Cassius Longinus Ravilla (consul 127 B.C.). When Cassius served as a trial judge, he reputedly asked this question frequently. (Cicero *In Defense of Sextus Roscius* 84; OCD s.v. Cassius Longinus Ravilla, Lucius)

### A gruesome consular first

Gnaeus Octavius, consul in 87 B.C. with Lucius Cornelius Cinna, had a falling out with his consular colleague, and expelled him from Rome. Cinna soon returned, however, reinforced by Gaius Marius and his adherents. They succeeded in capturing and decapitating Octavius, later displaying his severed head in the forum — the first time (but not the last) that a Roman consul was dishonored in such a fashion. (Appian *Civil Wars* 1.71)

### A last that resulted in a first

The last secession of the plebeians in 287 B.C. resulted in the appointment of the dictator Quintus Hortensius. He, in turn, passed legislation recognizing the legal status of plebiscites — a first — and thus persuading the plebeians to end the secession. (Livy *Epitome* 11; Pliny the Elder 16.37)

### Lucius Junius Brutus' firsts

Lucius Junius Brutus introduced a number of governmental reforms and practices (in 509 B.C.), including the taking of the auspices by newly elected officials, prior to their entry into office; an increase in the size of the Senate; the institution of the office of *rex sacrorum* ("king of sacred things"; the first holder of the office: Manlius Papirius). The holder of the latter office assumed the sacred duties of the kings after the dissolution of the monarchy. (MRR Vol. I 1)

### Nero's first act as emperor

Nero's first act as emperor (A.D. 54) was to inform his imperial guards that their password of the day would be "best mother," a tribute to Agrippina, his own mother. (Suetonius *Life of Nero* 10)

### Nero's first victim

Nero's long list of murder victims began with Claudius, his predecessor in the emperorship. Suetonius (*Life of Nero* 33) states that while Nero was not the actual murderer, he knew about the plot to poison Claudius, and did nothing to prevent it.

### New office holders under Augustus

Augustus created a number of new offices, to enable as many men as possible to participate in government. The new officials included those in charge of public buildings, roads, aqueducts, and the channel of the Tiber. (Suetonius *Life of Augustus* 37)

### The origins of the rivalry between Crassus and Pompey

According to Plutarch (*Life of Crassus* 6), the rivalry between Crassus and Pompey first began during the turmoil of the 80s B.C., when both men courted Sulla's approval. Sulla seemed to prefer Pompey, which aroused feelings of jealousy in Crassus.

### The political firsts of Publius Cornelius Lentulus Spinther

In a lengthy letter to Cicero (*Letters to Friends* 12.14), Publius Cornelius Lentulus Spinther details his accomplishments as the governor of Asia in 44 and 43 B.C. He claims to have been the first to do the following: (1) ignore certain of Mark Antony's laws regarding various Asian provinces; (2) transfer Publius Cornelius Dolabella's cavalry to republican armies (43 B.C.), and the first to secure Syria for Cassius; (3) "declare war on all my friends and family," a reference to his opposition to Dolabella (and by extension, Antony), his erstwhile allies.

### The political firsts of Quintus Publilius Philo

The noted plebeian politician Quintus Publilius Philo (consul 339, 327, 320, 315 B.C.) is credited with three firsts: (1) He was the first plebeian praetor (337); he was the first man to hold proconsular powers (326); (3) he promulgated a series of laws (the *Publiliae leges*), one of which gave the plebeians legitimate political clout for the first time, by freeing the centuriate assembly from senatorial constraints. (Boren 29; Harper's s.v. Philo [7])

### Pompey's consular firsts

When Pompey gained his sole consulship in 52 B.C., it marked the first time in Roman history that so many powers and access to so much money, and to the Roman army, had been legally conferred on any holder of that office. (Appian *Civil Wars* 1.23)

### The repeated use of the first word

Cicero describes an oratorical technique — epanaphora — in which a series of sentences or clauses begin with the same word. Example: *Scipio Numantiam sustulit; Scipio Kartaginem delevit; Scipio pacem peperit; Scipio civitatem servavit.* ("Scipio razed Numantia, Scipio destroyed Carthage, Scipio brought peace, Scipio saved the state." tr. Caplan [LCL] 277). In the same passage Cicero notes that orators may also employ the opposite technique — antistrophe — in which the final word in a series of clauses or sentences is repeated. (Cicero *To Gaius Herennius* 4.19)

### Rome's first foreign king

After a reconciliation had been brought about between the Romans and the Sabines (after the celebrated kidnapping of the Sabine women), Romulus and the Sabine king Titus Tatius became corulers, thus making Tatius the first nonnative king of Rome. (OCD s.v. Tatius)

## Category Three
# Firsts in Military and Foreign Affairs

### Greek

*The dangers of the first crossing of the Nile*

When the Macedonian king Perdiccas III invaded Egypt in 321 B.C., his soldiers experienced some unexpected difficulties in crossing the Nile. Since the current was strong, Perdiccas posted two lines of mounted soldiers from one bank to the other. Those upstream sat upon elephants, whose bulk helped to break the current; downstream, horsemen were assigned the task of rescuing any soldiers who had been swept away, elephants notwithstanding.

The first group of soldiers waded across to the far bank relatively unharmed, but the rest were not so lucky. The first ones to ford the river had disturbed its sandy bottom, with the result that much of the sand was either compressed or carried downstream. Hence, the newly deepened river became more difficult to cross. Perdiccas ordered his remaining men to swim; but many of them, being poor swimmers, either drowned or fell prey to crocodiles. Some 2,000 soldiers were lost in this way. (Diodorus Siculus 18.35–36)

*Dionysiac firsts*

Dionysius I, fourth century B.C. tyrant of Syracuse, was noted for several military innovations, facilitated by his policy of hiring the best engineers and craftsmen.

1. Reputedly the first catapult was perfected during his regime.
2. He initiated the construction of quadriremes and quinqueremes (ships with four and five banks of oars, respectively). He was partially motivated to expand his fleet in this way because military engineers in the rival city of Corinth had first invented triremes. (Diodorus Siculus 14.42)

Dionysius has been called "the first of the Romantic 'great men'; the precursor of Alexander the Great, Hannibal, and Napoleon..." (OCD s.v. Dionysius I [1])

### The first alliance

The Peloponnesian League, formed in the sixth century B.C. and consisting of Sparta and its allies, is generally considered to have been the first alliance of Greek polises with mutual foreign policy interests. (OCD s.v. alliance [Greek])

### The first Athenian to capture a Persian warship

The first Athenian admiral to capture a Persian ship at the Battle of Salamis was Lycomedes. This Lycomedes, commander of a trireme, later removed the ship's figurehead and dedicated it to Apollo. (Plutarch *Life of Themistocles* 10)

### The first attempted secession from the Delian League

The first Delian League member to attempt to secede from the League (formed circa 478 B.C.) was Naxos, in 467. The Athenians quelled the uprising, and maintained their hegemony over the island. (OCD s.v. Naxos)

### The first Delian League assessment

The Athenian Aristides drew up the first assessments to be exacted from the members of the mutual defense alliance known as the Delian League (circa 478 B.C.) The annual tribute amounted to 460 talents, payable to the Athenians, who would presumably use the funding to maintain their fleets and to ward off future Persian invasions. (Plutarch *Life of Aristides* 24; OCD s.v. Delian League)

### The first Greek colony in Italy

The Euboeans founded Cumae, the first Greek colony in Italy, around 740 B.C. (OCD s.v. Cumae)

### The first military accomplishment of the Delian League

Shortly after its formation circa 478 B.C., the Delian League moved against Persian strongholds in Thrace. The league's first victory in this campaign was the capture of Eion, in 476. (CAH V 50)

### The first military "think tank"

Dionysius I, tyrant of Syracuse, created the first "think tank" by recruiting the best weapons designers and craftsmen and assigning them the task of producing a cache of first rate weapons; he planned to use the weaponry in an assault on Carthaginian strongholds in Sicily. The craftsmen came from Italy, Greece and even Carthage itself.

Dionysius was also apparently the first person to conceive of warships outfitted with four and five banks of oars; previous designs had a maximum of three. (Diodorus Siculus 14.41.3–4)

### The first non–Greek city ruled by Athens

When the Athenians established hegemony over Sigeum (in modern northwestern Turkey) in the seventh century B.C., it became the first city they ruled which was not located on the Greek mainland. (OCD s.v. Sigeum)

### The first place for bravery

After the Battle of Salamis, the victorious Greek generals took a vote to determine which of them should take first place for bravery. When the ballots were tabulated, it was discovered that each general had voted himself the bravest, with Themistocles second. (Plutarch *Life of Themistocles* 17)

### The first to flee the Battle of Salamis

The Phoenicians were the first Persian contingent to flee from the Battle of Salamis (480 B.C.). Those whom Xerxes caught, he executed; the rest made their way first to Attica, with Asia their ultimate goal. (Diodorus Siculus 11.19)

### A recruit's first defeat

Prior to the decisive battle in Sicily against the Spartans, the Athenian commander Nicias made a speech to the troops, in which he urged them to press forward courageously, and not become discouraged. Especially to be avoided was the instinct of many raw recruits who, if they taste defeat in their first experience in combat, are thenceforward plagued by fears that every subsequent battle will have the same result.

Prior to the same battle, the Spartan commander Gylippus also addressed his soldiers. Among other things, he reminded them that they had been "the first men who ever withstood [the Athenian] fleet." (Thucydides 7.61; 66; tr. Smith Vol. IV [LCL])

### A Spartan king's first duty before battle

Before leading an army into battle, a Spartan king first sacrificed to the Muses, probably to remind himself and his soldiers of their Spartan upbringing and education, and also to motivate them to perform in a manner worthy of being recorded by historians and poets. (Plutarch *Life of Lycurgus* 21)

### Themistocles' first act as commander

When Themistocles assumed command of Athens' fleet (circa 481 B.C.), he first ordered all the citizens to board triremes and to engage the oncoming Persians in a sea battle, as far distant from Athens as possible. (Plutarch *Life of Themistocles* 7)

### Three Carian military innovations

Herodotus (1.171) notes that the Greeks copied three Carian military innovations: the wearing of crested helmets; the use of devices on shields; the equipping of shields with holsters for the arm.

## Roman

### Ariminum's firsts

As a town on the northern frontier of Italy, Ariminum was the first to witness invading Gauls (the Senones in 390 B.C., the Cimbrians and Teutones in 101) and Carthaginians, in 218. (Lucan *Civil War* 1)

### Cato the Elder's first military experience

Cato the Elder was only 17 years of age when he was thrust into the heat of battle at the siege of Capua, during the Second Punic War. (Harper's s.v. Cato [1])

### Crassus' first mistake

Marcus Licinius Crassus' first mistake as the commander of the Parthian War (54–53 B.C.) was his failure to press an attack immediately upon his arrival in the area. Plutarch (*Life of Crassus* 17) notes sarcastically that actually, Crassus' first and biggest blunder was initiating a war at all against the Parthians.

### A dispute over the first to climb the wall

The first man to scale a town's walls during an assault was generally honored with a mural crown (*muralis corona*). In 210 B.C., after the capture of New Carthage, an unseemly dispute arose between two petitioners for the crown: Quintus Trebellius and Sextus Digitius. A special arbitration panel was appointed to resolve the matter. After a lengthy debate, the arbiters determined that the two men had surmounted the wall simultaneously; hence, they decreed that each man should receive a crown. (Livy 26.48)

Alexander the Great also attached significance to being the first to scale an enemy's wall; Appian (*Civil Wars* 2.149) relates an anecdote about an occasion on which Alexander climbed an enemy's rampart alone, receiving 13 wounds for his efforts.

### Euphranor's fatal first

The first century B.C. Rhodian naval commander Euphranor was noted for his aggressive battle tactics, which were almost always successful. But at the Battle of Canopus (near Alexandria), he met his end, when his was (as usual) the first ship to attack and sink an Alexandrian vessel. Perhaps overly jubilant after the initial success, he pursued another enemy ship, but failed to allow sufficient time for the rest of his fleet to accompany him; this enabled the Alexandrians to encircle and sink Euphranor's ship. (Julius Caesar *Alexandrian War* 25)

### A first and last of Aulus Plautius

Aulus Plautius was the first consular governor of Britain, in the first century A.D. He was the last Roman general to celebrate a minor triumphal procession (*ovatio*). (Tacitus *Life of Agricola* 14; OCD s.v. Plautius)

### The first benefit of soldiering

According to Juvenal (16.7–9), the most significant of the many soldiering perquisites was the soldier's immunity to civilian laws and punishments.

### The first cause of the hostility between Marius and Sulla

According to Plutarch (*Life of Marius* 10), the hostility between Gaius Marius and Lucius Cornelius Sulla first arose over an incident in Africa, in which Jugurtha was treacherously handed over to Sulla. Sulla thus claimed the credit for capturing Jugurtha and ending his instigations of violence and rebellion; Marius believed that the glory for quashing Jugurtha was more appropriately due to him than to Sulla.

### The first combined triumph

Lesser triumphs (*ovationes*) were not celebrated simultaneously with triumphs proper (*triumphi*). However, when Tiberius concelebrated an *ovatio* and a *triumphus* (circa 7 B.C., for victories in Germany and Gaul), it marked the first time that such an honor had been granted to any Roman military leader. (Suetonius *Life of Tiberius* 9)

### The first consul killed by Roman soldiers

Quintus Pompeius, one of the consuls for 88 B.C.— the other was Sulla, was killed by Roman soldiers during a military mutiny, the first time that a consul met his death at the hands of Roman legionnaires. (Velleius Paterculus 2.20)

### The first display to the Parthians of Roman power

The first direct encounter with Roman military power which the Parthians experienced occurred in the 90s B.C., when Lucius Cornelius Sulla became the provincial governor of Cilicia. (OCD s.v. Cornelius Sulla Felix, Lucius)

*The first eastern incursion by Rome*

In 201 B.C., the Romans first became involved in eastern affairs when they joined with the Rhodians in an action against Philip V and Antiochus. (OCD s.v. Rhodes)

*The first emperor to bribe the soldiers*

According to Suetonius (*Life of Claudius* 10), when the emperor Claudius promised a per capita largesse of 15,000 sesterces to the army to gain its loyalty, it marked the first time that an emperor had ever attempted to bribe the military in this fashion.

*The first equestrian to receive a mural crown*

The first Roman equestrian to receive a mural crown (awarded to the first soldier to scale an enemy's wall in battle) was Marcus Manlius Capitolinus, in the fourth century B.C. (Pliny the Elder 7.103)

*The first examples of decline in the Roman army*

According to Sallust (*War with Catiline* 11), Lucius Cornelius Sulla was responsible for the first serious decline of Roman military discipline. When he led the troops into Asia, he allowed them great freedom to behave as they wished in their off-duty hours. Hence, it was then that the legions "first learned to indulge in women and drink; to admire statues, paintings and ... vases, to steal them from private houses and public places, to pillage shrines, and to desecrate everything..." (tr. Rolfe [LCL] 21)

*The first foreign invasion of Italy*

In 280 B.C., when the Epirote king Pyrrhus invaded Tarentum, it marked the first time that a foreign invader had entered Roman Italy. (*Oxford History of the Classical World* 404–405)

*The first formal Roman provincial boundary*

The first Roman *limes*—clearly delineated provincial boundary—was established by the emperor Hadrian in Germany, circa A.D. 121, in the form of a wooden wall. Previously, boundaries had been marked less formally, often by military roads. (OCD s.vv. Hadrian; *limes*)

*The first freedmen in the Roman army*

The first time that enrollment of freedmen in the Roman army occurred was during the Social War, around 89 B.C. (Livy *Epitome* 74)

*The first general sent against Spartacus*

When Spartacus initiated his famous slave/gladiator uprising in 73 B.C., official Rome underestimated the seriousness of the situation. The first commander sent to southern Italy to deal with Spartacus was Varinius Glaber; he did not even have a trained army at his disposal, but soldiers haphazardly recruited and formed into an irregular unit. Spartacus and his adherents defeated this military medley, even seizing Varinius' horse in the process, "so narrowly did the very general of the Romans escape being captured by a gladiator." (Appian *Civil Wars* 1.116; tr. White Vol. III [LCL])

### The first general to award a gold crown

Pliny the Elder (33.38), following Lucius Calpurnius Piso, writes that the first general to award a gold crown for bravery to a soldier was Aulus Postumius Albus, after the Battle of Lake Regillus, circa 497 B.C.

### The first general to celebrate an ovation

Publius Postumius Tubertus was the first Roman general to celebrate an *ovatio* (small-scale triumphal procession) within the city of Rome, around 503 B.C. Hence, he established the precedent of wearing a myrtle wreath on such occasions. The first and only general to depart from this tradition: Marcus Licinius Crassus, who wore a laurel wreath during the celebration for his victory over Spartacus, in 71 B.C. (Pliny the Elder 15.126)

### The first general to display elephants in a triumphal procession

Lucius Caecilius Metellus, consul in 251 B.C., was the first Roman general to include elephants in a triumphal procession; he had captured the animals in the First Punic War, at the Battle of Panormus.

He transported these elephants — some 140 — from Africa to Rome on rafts constructed of barrels tied together and overlaid with planking (Pliny the Elder 8.16, where Pliny also states that the first triumphal procession featuring elephants occurred in 275 B.C., thus contradicting his statement in 7.139, where he suggests a date of about 250 B.C. for this elephantine first).

Metellus subsequently enjoyed a signal honor: he was granted permission to be conveyed to the Senate house in a chariot, the first and only Roman so privileged. He had lost his eyesight, so the story goes, while rescuing a sacred statue from the burning Temple of Vesta; in gratitude for that selfless act, and to compensate for his blindness, the Romans gave him the right to ride to the Senate. (Pliny the Elder 7.139, 141; OCD s.v. Caecilius Metellus, Lucius)

### First in the generalship rankings

A (probably fictitious) meeting once took place between Hannibal and his Roman conqueror, Scipio Africanus. Scipio asked him which general in history he would consider the best ever; Hannibal named Alexander the Great. Scipio did not disagree, but then inquired which general would be second.

That honor would go to Pyrrhus, Hannibal replied, because Pyrrhus possessed the first quality necessary for effective generalship: boldness.

By now, Scipio was wondering where he might fit in this emerging hierarchy. So he asked once again, this time about third place. Hannibal rated himself third, in part because he was the first mortal general ever to lead an army over the Alps Mountains. Hannibal went on to say that he would have ranked himself first, had he been able to defeat Scipio in battle. (Appian *Syrian Wars* 10)

### The first invasion of Rome — by a Roman general

When Lucius Cornelius Sulla led an attack on the city of Rome in 82 B.C., it represented the first time that a Roman general had ever initiated such an assault. (Boren 107)

### The first lowly plebeians in the Roman army

In the early years of Roman history, the ranks of the army were filled by those who met certain property qualifications. But in the late second century B.C., Gaius Marius set a precedent by enrolling plebeians who were in some cases living in near poverty conditions. (Boren 99)

### The first messenger to Tigranes: hanged

When the Roman commander Lucius Licinius Lucullus was preparing to attack Tigranes (69 B.C.), that noted Armenian king hanged the first messenger who brought him the news. (Appian *Mithridatic Wars* 84)

### The first naval victory over the Carthaginians

Gaius Duilius (consul in 260 B.C.) defeated the Carthaginians and the Sicilians in the naval Battle of Mylae in 260, and subsequently celebrated the first naval triumph. The victory was facilitated by the first practical use of the *corvus*, a device similar to a gangplank; in close quarters, the Romans extended *corvi* to the enemy ships and boarded them. (OCD s.v. Duilius)

### The first novus homo to earn a military cognomen

After the *novus homo* Lucius Mummius led the successful assault on Corinth in 146 B.C., he was given the honorary cognomen Achaicus. This marked the first time in Roman history that a new man was so honored. (Velleius Paterculus 1.13)

### The first Parthian hostages seen in Rome

Augustus displayed the first Parthian hostages ever seen in Rome, during one of his public shows. He personally paraded them through the middle of the arena, and then seated them near him to view the games. (Suetonius *Life of Augustus* 43)

*The first Parthian king*

The Parthians, longtime rivals of the Romans, were ruled by a series of kings, all of whom adopted the title Arsaces, the name of the first Parthian king (who reigned in the third century B.C.). (Williams *Cicero: The Letters to His Friends* Vol. II [LCL] 166)

*The first pay for soldiers*

According to tradition, Roman soldiers first received payment for their efforts during the siege of Veii (circa 406–396 B.C.). This was also the first time that the Roman military had engaged in siege warfare. (Boren 36)

*The first plebeian general to conduct a military campaign*

A few years after plebeian eligibility for the consulship was ratified, a plebeian consul faced the prospect of becoming the first of his social class to lead an army into battle; the date was 362 B.C. The enemy were the Hernici, the consul, Lucius Genucius. All Rome waited anxiously to learn the outcome of this plebeian first. Genucius led the army into an ambush; the soldiers fled, and Genucius was killed. When the news reached Rome, the patricians displayed unseemly joy, for in their minds, the incident proved that plebeians were incapable of high office or public responsibility. (Livy 7.6)

*The first Pontic king friendly to Rome*

The first Pontic king to be a "friend of the Roman people" was Mithridates V (Euergetes), who reigned from approximately 156 to 120 B.C. (Appian *Mithridatic Wars* 10; tr. White Vol. II [LCL] 255)

*The first public wearing of crowns*

In 292 B.C., individuals who had won military crowns for bravery in battle were for the first time permitted to wear their crowns at the Roman games. In the same year, the custom of presenting victorious charioteers with palms was begun. (Livy 10.47)

*The first reference to the speaker's platform as the rostra*

The speaker's platform in the forum was first adorned by the prows — *rostra* — of captured enemy ships in 338 B.C. A naval victory over the people of Antium in this year was the event which resulted in the instituting of this custom. (Livy 8.14; Pliny the Elder 34.20)

*The first Roman general to cross the Taurus*

Dio (36.16) states that Lucius Licinius Lucullus was the first Roman general to lead an army across the Taurus River for battle.

*The first Roman general to cross to Sicily*

The first Roman military leader to cross over from Italy to Sicily with a fleet was the consul Claudius Caudex (264 B.C.). He subsequently expelled the Carthaginians from Sicily. (Suetonius *Life of Tiberius* 2; MRR Vol. I 202–203)

*The first Roman general to defeat Hannibal*

According to Livy (26.29), Marcus Claudius Marcellus was the first Roman general to gain a clear-cut military victory over Hannibal (210 B.C.); unfortunately, the historian provides no details about the matter.

*The first Roman general to sail to the northern ocean*

Decimus Claudius Drusus (the father of the emperor Claudius) was the first Roman general to lead a fleet to the *oceanus septionalis*, the "northern ocean." (Suetonius *Life of Claudius* 1)

*The first Roman governor of Syria*

According to Appian (*Syrian War* 51), the first Roman governor to administer the province of Syria with an army was Aulus Gabinius, around 56 B.C.

*The first Roman troops in Spain*

Roman soldiers first appeared in Spain in 218 B.C., with Gnaeus Cornelius Scipio as the commander. (Velleius Paterculus 2.90)

*The first tasks in setting up and breaking camp*

When the Roman army was on the march, and a camp was deemed necessary, the first consideration was locating a suitable site for the consul's tent. His tent, and those of the tribunes, were always the first ones to be pitched.

When the army was ready to break camp, the striking of the tents was the first task. The first tents to be taken down were those belonging to the consul and the tribunes. (Polybius 6.27, 40, 41)

*The first to climb the ladder at New Carthage*

When Scipio Africanus was preparing his army for an attack on New Carthage in 209 B.C., he observed that a lagoon (which abutted the southern wall of the city) could be crossed at low tide. So he urged his men to make their assault at that time; he himself was in the forefront, and was the first to reach the wall, place a ladder against it, and begin the climb. (Appian *Wars in Spain* 21–22; OCD s.v. Cornelius Scipio Africanus [the Elder], Publius)

*The first to enter Carthage (146 B.C.)*

Although the Roman victory in the Third Punic War is most frequently associated with Scipio Aemilianus, the "first to force an entrance into Carthage" was the naval commander Lucius Hostilius Mancinus. (Pliny the Elder 35.23; tr. Rackham Vol. IX [LCL] 277)

### The first to enter the battlefield, and the last to leave

Livy (21.4) asserts that the Carthaginian general Hannibal was always the first to appear on the field of battle, and the last to depart.

### The first to enter the Rubicon

When Julius Caesar made his fateful crossing of the Rubicon River in 49 B.C., the first portion of the army to proceed was the cavalry. They stationed themselves in the river to break the current, thus facilitating the crossing for the rest of the army. (Lucan *Civil War* 1)

### The first to flee Actium

According to Velleius Paterculus (2.85), Cleopatra was the first leader of note to flee from the Battle of Actium. Velleius remarks contemptuously that Mark Antony followed her, rather than remaining with the army.

### The first to give the battle signal at Pharsalus

The prelude to the Battle of Pharsalus (48 B.C.) was marked by introspection and sorrow on both sides, for this was the first time in Roman history that two Italian armies of such magnitude would face each other in battle. After much hesitation, Pompey gave the signal to begin hostilities. The first weapons employed were arrows and stones, launched prior to the hand-to-hand combat. (Appian *Civil Wars* 2.77–78)

### The first to recognize Gaul's strategic significance

Marcus Aemilius Lepidus (consul 78 B.C.) was "the first to realize the strategic importance of an unified province of Gaul." (OCD s.v. Aemilius Lepidus [3])

### The first to sleep on straw

When Publius Cornelius Scipio Aemilianus was given the responsibility in 133 B.C. of bringing to a conclusion a war against Numantia (Spain) that had been dragging on for years, he decided that his first step would be to restore discipline in the army. He began by evicting camp followers (e.g., entrepreneurs of various sorts, including prostitutes), reducing the nonmilitary equipment to the barest essentials, restricting the soldiers' diets to the simplest fare, and replacing their comfortable beds with straw matting. A leader by example, he was the first one to sleep on the straw.

When Scipio ordered the circumvallation of Numantia, it was (in Appian's opinion) most likely the first time that a city whose men did not fear open warfare had been blockaded in such a manner. (Appian *Wars in Spain* 84–85; 91)

### The first to subdue Britain

The first Roman military commander to completely subjugate Britain was Gnaeus Julius Agricola. Agricola was also the first — and only — senator known to have held important imperial posts on three different occasions in the same province (Britain): military tribune A.D. 60–61; legionary commander 71–73; governor 77–84.

Under Agricola's leadership, the first Roman circumnavigation of the island was completed. (Tacitus *Life of Agricola* 10; OCD s.v. Julius Agricola, Gnaeus)

### The first to support Galba

The first consequential Roman to support Galba's insurrection against Nero was Otho; Otho hated Nero because of a disagreement over the affections of Nero's mistress, Poppaea Sabina. (Suetonius *Life of Otho* 3)

### The first to wound an elephant at Zama

At the decisive Battle of Zama (202 B.C., between Rome and Carthage), the Carthaginians almost immediately deployed their elephants. The first Roman to dismount from his horse and wound an elephant was none other than the commanding general himself, Publius Cornelius Scipio Africanus. (Appian *Punic Wars* 43)

### Flaminius' firsts

Gaius Flaminius (consul 223, 217) was the first governor of Sicily (MRR Vol. I 229); later (in 223), he became the first general to lead an army across the Po River, in northern Italy. He was also "the [first and] only politician before the Gracchi to mount a serious challenge to the senatorial establishment on behalf of the *populares*." (OCD s.v. Flaminius [1], Gaius)

### Gaius Marius' first military service

Gaius Marius' first military service took place in Spain, in 134 B.C., in a campaign against the Celtiberians. (Plutarch *Life of Marius* 3)

### Hamilcar Barca's first son

The first son of the Carthaginian general Hamilcar Barca was the more renowned general, Hannibal. (OCD s.v. Hannibal)

*Juba's firsts*

King Juba II (died circa A.D. 23), the first to rule over both Mauretanias (East and West) was, according to Pliny the Elder (5.16), even more noted for his scholarship than for his regality. It is said that he invented Gaetulian purple, a kind of dye, and that he was the first to study and apply the benefits of a plant called euphorbia, whose juice was claimed to have been an antidote to poisons and an aid to vision. (OCD s.v. Juba [2] II)

*Jugurthine firsts*

The Numidian king Jugurtha was no stay-at-home ruler. He often competed with his friends and his subjects in contests such as foot racing and javelin throwing. When he went on lion hunts, he was often the first, or one of the first, hunters to find and slay a lion. (Sallust *Jugurtha* 6)

*Nero's military priorities*

When preparing to lead a military expedition against the Gauls, Nero's first priority was to ensure that his theatrical props were loaded into the wagons. At the same time, he ordered his prostitutes — all of whom were to accompany him — to cut their hair and attire themselves like soldiers. (Suetonius *Life of Nero* 44)

*The self-claimed firsts of Publius Cornelius Lentulus Spinther (the Younger)*

Publius Cornelius Lentulus Spinther, a provincial governor in Asia in the 40s B.C., claimed for himself several firsts:

1. He was the first politician of note to flout and disregard the *leges Antoniae*, "laws of (Mark) Antony," respecting Asia.
2. After the suicide of the volatile Publius Cornelius Dolabella in 43, Lentulus was the first to transfer the command of Dolabella's troops to Gaius Cassius Longinus.
3. He was the first to oppose militarily the allies of his former friend and associate Dolabella.

Lentulus also mentions that he was the first to raise an army to combat an (unspecified) "most nefarious conspiracy" (tr. Williams). (Cicero *The Letters to Friends* 12.14 [a letter actually written by Lentulus to Cicero]; Williams Vol. II [LCL] 556–557)

*Two African firsts*

The Roman army first conducted military campaigns in Mauretania during the reign of the emperor Claudius (A.D. 41–54). The first Roman general to lead an army into and beyond the Atlas Mountain range was Suetonius Paulinus (consul in A.D. 66, and the father of the biographer Suetonius). He provided detailed accounts of the flora, fauna and geographical features he encountered. (Pliny the Elder 5.14–15; Rackham Vol. II [LCL] 228)

### A war horse's first tasks

Horses bred for war must first of all be taught the following: to observe weaponry; to endure trumpet blasts and the creaking of chariot wheels; to hear the sounds of bits and bridles while still in the stable. (Vergil *Georgics* 3.179–184)

# Firsts in Art, Architecture, Literature, Science

## Greek

*Aeschylus' first dramatic victory*

The first victory in the dramatic competitions for a play by Aeschylus occurred in 484 B.C., although neither the play itself nor its title is extant. His first extant play, *The Persians*, was performed in 472. Aeschylus competed for the first time in 500 B.C. (OCD s.v. Aeschylus)

*Agathon's first dramatic victory*

The tragic playwright Agathon first attained victory in the dramatic competitions in 416 B.C., while he was still in his 20s. The title and content of his winning play are unknown, although his victory was commemorated in Plato's *Symposium*, a social gathering to celebrate Agathon's success. Agathon is also said to have been the first playwright to compose choral interludes having no relevance to the play's storyline. (Aristotle *Poetics* 18; OCD s.v. Agathon)

*Anaximenes' firsts*

Anaximenes of Miletus (fl. sixth century B.C.), a student of Anaximander, was the first to elucidate "the theory of shadows and the science called gnomonics," and the first to display in Sparta "the time-piece they call 'Hunt-the-Shadow' [*sciothericon*]." (Pliny the Elder 2.187; tr. Rackham Vol. I [LCL] 319)

### Apollodorus' firsts

Apollodorus of Athens (fifth century B.C.) "was the first artist to give realistic presentation of objects, and the first to confer glory as of right upon the paintbrush." He was also the first to employ shading techniques in his paintings. Pliny asserts that no artist prior to Apollodorus could so effectively rivet the attention of those admiring his work. (Pliny the Elder 35.60; tr. Rackham Vol. IX [LCL] 306, 307)

### Aristophanes' dramatic firsts

Aristophanes' first comic play *Daitaleis (Banqueters)* was performed in 427 B.C.; it is not extant. His earliest surviving play, *Acharnians* (425) won the first prize in the dramatic competitions. (Harper's s.v. Aristophanes)

### Athens' first resident philosopher

Anaxagoras (circa 500–428 B.C.) was "the first philosopher known to have settled in Athens." It is thought that he came to Athens around 455; later, he became a friend and tutor of Pericles. (OCD s.v. Anaxagoras)

### The author of the first Herculean epic

The first known epic poem about Hercules was authored by Pisander of Camirus (Rhodes), who flourished in the seventh or sixth century B.C. (OCD s.v. Pisander [1])

### Butades' firsts

Butades of Corinth was responsible for a number of artistic inventions and innovations:

1. He was the first to create clay models for use in portraiture.
2. He devised various methods of producing clay to use in the modelling.
3. He was the first to design and produce decorative tiles for roof gutters; this, in turn, served as the inspiration for pedimental decoration in temples. (Pliny the Elder 35.151, 152)

### Eratosthenes' firsts

Eratosthenes (circa 275–194 B.C.) was the first author to compile a geographical survey of the known world, and he was also the first to calculate the earth's circumference. He determined that the distance from Alexandria to the city of Syene was two percent of the true circumference; from that assumption, he arrived at a figure which has proven to be accurate within one percent.

The epithet *Philologus* ("word lover," by extension, one who loves words in a context, and hence, a learned scholar) was first claimed by Eratosthenes. (Lesky 786–787; OCD s.v. Eratosthenes)

*Euclidean firsts*

Euclid founded the first school of mathematics in Alexandria. And while he was not the first Greek mathematician, he does claim the distinction of being the first to systematize the form and study of mathematics, especially geometry. (Harper's s.v. Euclid [2])

*Euripides' dramatic firsts*

Euripides competed in the dramatic contests for the first time in 455 B.C.; he won for the first time in 441. (Harper's s.v. Euripides)

*The first advocate of the heliocentric theory*

The third century B.C. astronomer Aristarchus of Samos was the first to suggest that the earth revolved around the sun. Parmenides (fl. fifth century B.C.) reputedly first advanced the theory that a spherical earth was located at the center of the universe. (OCD s.v. geocentricity)

*The first air pressure devices*

The third century B.C. Alexandrian inventor Ctesibius was the first to construct mechanical devices which functioned by air pressure. These contrivances included pumps, water-clocks, water-organs, and catapults. (Vitruvius 9.2; OCD s.v. Ctesibius)

*A first and last of Philochorus*

The erudite Philochorus (circa 340–260 B.C.) has been called "the first scholar" (Jacoby, quoted in OCD) to compose a localized history of Attica (*Atthis*); other representatives of the genre had appeared before Philochorus' version, but apparently none as scholarly. Ironically, he was also the last noted author to produce an *atthis*. Hellanicus of Lesbos (fl. fifth century B.C.) is regarded as the first composer of an *atthis*. (OCD s.vv. Hellanicus; Philochorus)

*The first and only complete Sapphic poem*

Most of Sappho's poetry is fragmentary. The only complete poem is also the first one in the corpus, a prayer to Aphrodite. (Hadas 52)

*The first and only Greek tragedy to feature an Olympian deity*

Sophocles' *Ajax* is the first and only known Greek tragedy in which an Olympian deity — in this case, Athena — plays a prominent role in the plot. She is, in fact, the first character to speak in the play. (Lesky 276)

*The first animal biologist*

Aristotle's studies of animals, and his treatises about them, are the earliest

and putatively the best work done on the subject in antiquity. (OCD s.v. animals, knowledge about)

### The first artist to create a plaster life-mask

Lysistratus of Sicyon (fl. fourth century B.C.) was the first portrait artist to create plaster life-masks. The method which he devised for producing these masks involved "pouring wax into ... plaster mould[s] and then making final corrections on the wax cast." He also invented a way to create likenesses from statues, and using these likenesses as models for portraiture. (Pliny the Elder 35.153; tr. Rackham Vol. IX [LCL] 373)

### The first artist to portray male and female differences

The first artist to differentiate male and female subjects (not anatomically, but by depicting the females with paler skin) was Eumarus of Athens. Cimon of Cleonae improved upon Eumarus' methods, and also invented *catagrapha*, "images in three-quarter."

Cimon was the first to bestow a sort of three-dimensional quality to his paintings, by giving the subjects a variety of poses. He was also the first artist to portray folds in the clothing worn by the subjects. (Pliny the Elder 35.56; tr. Rackham Vol. IX [LCL] 302, 303)

### The first artist to understand the potential of sculpting

According to Pliny the Elder (34.54), the fifth century B.C. artist/sculptor Phidias was thought to have been the "first [to reveal] the capabilities and [the first to indicate] the methods of statuary." (tr. Rackham Vol. IX [LCL] 167)

### The first artist trained in arithmetic and geometry

The fourth century B.C. Macedonian Pamphilus was the first artist trained in many fields of study, including arithmetic and geometry which, he claimed, were essential components in the quest for artistic perfection. He charged his art students — including the celebrated painter Apelles of Cos — the astronomical sum of one talent for a 12-year art course.

He was also the first artist to train young children to paint by having them create sketches on boxwood panels. (Pliny the Elder 35.76–77; OCD s.v. Pamphilus [1])

### The first astrological writer

Berosus (fl. third century B.C.), an immigrant to Cos and founder of a school there, was said by Vitruvius (9.6) to have been the first Greek writer on astrology.

*The first Athenian poet*

Although better known as a statesman and diplomat, Solon also wrote poetry, the first Athenian to engage in this literary activity. (Lesky 122)

*The first author to speculate about lifespans*

In one of Hesiod's lost works, he delves into the question of life expectancies, not only for humans, but also for various animals, including crows, ravens, and deer. According to Pliny the Elder (7.153), Hesiod was the first author to study and describe such matters.

*The first author to write about music*

Lasus of Athens (fl. sixth century B.C.) was the first author to compose a book on music (now lost). He also initiated contests for dithyrambic poets in Athens, around 508 B.C. (OCD s.v. Lasus)

*The first book collector*

According to Strabo (reference in Sandys 19), Aristotle was the first person to collect books, thus serving as a model for the kings of Egypt, noted as founders and patrons of the great libraries at Alexandria.

*The first book on alchemy*

The author of the first book on alchemy (*Natural and Initiatory Matters*) is thought to have been Democritus. (OCD s.v. alchemy)

*The first book on Greek grammar*

Dionysius of Thrace (circa 170–90 B.C.) compiled the earliest known book on Greek grammar. Although less than 16 pages in length, its authoritative influence extended well into the medieval period. (Sandys 44–45)

*The first book on the history of civilization*

The first author to attempt to write a survey on the history of civilization was Dicaearchus of Messana (fl. 310 B.C.). His treatise was entitled *Bios tes Hellas, Life of Greece.* (Sandys 27)

*The first botanical writer*

Menestor (fl. fifth century B.C.), who wrote several books about plants, was "the author of the first known Greek works on inductive botany." (OCD s.v. Menestor)

*The first choral lyrics*

The first choral lyrics and lyricists (e.g., Alcman and Tyrtaeus) first flourished in Sparta, in the seventh century B.C. (Harper's s.v. Sparta)

### The first city planner

According to Aristotle (*Politics* 2), Hippodamus of Miletus was the first to utilize the grid plan in designing the layout of city streets (although the current view holds that Hippodamus did not invent the system, but rather the methods for its implementation.) Aristotle also attributes to him the distinction of being the first non-politician to define the characteristics of the best kind of constitution.

### The first comic poet

Aristotle (*Poetics* 4.12) credits Homer with the distinction of being the first comic poet, since he established the foundation of the genre through his satirical poems (e.g., *Margites*).

### The first comic poet to "generalize his dialogue and plots"

According to Aristotle (*Poetics* 5.6), Crates was the first Athenian comic poet to remove personal attacks and lampoons from his plays, and to "generalize his dialogue and plots." (tr. Fyfe [Aristotle *Poetics* in LCL] 21)

### The first Corinthian capital

Vitruvius (4.1.9–10) relates an interesting story about the first Corinthian capital. A young Corinthian girl was struck down by disease in the bloom of her youth and died. Her nurse gathered together the girl's collection of goblets and placed them in a basket covered by a roof tile; she then placed the basket on top of the girl's tomb. By chance, an acanthus root was directly beneath the basket; when the plant began to grow and blossom, its leaves and branches grew alongside the sides of the basket, while the weight of the tile forced the shoots to curl at their ends.

An architect by the name of Callimachus, who happened to pass by the tomb, observed the pattern created by the leaves growing around the basket. He was so intrigued by the sight that he designed column capitals which imitated it; hence, the creation of the acanthus leaf motif, the outstanding characteristic of a Corinthian column.

### The first datable Greek prose writing

A Nubian inscription made by Greek mercenary soldiers in 589 B.C. stands as the first known Greek prose writing to which a specific date may be assigned. (Hadas 65)

### The first delineator of moods and genders

The first writer to have noted the distinctions of mood in verbs and gender in nouns was reputedly Pythagoras of Abdera. (Harper's s.v. Pythagoras)

*The first editions of Pindar and Aristophanes*
Aristophanes of Byzantium was the first ancient scholar to collate and edit the odes of Pindar and the plays of Aristophanes (the comic poet). He also seems to have been the first critic to organize the fifteen dialogues of Plato into sets of three. (OCD s.v. Aristophanes of Byzantium)

*The first epigrammatic anthology*
Meleager of Syria (fl. circa 100 B.C.) compiled the first anthology of epigrams. Called the *Garland*, it was comprised of work by an array of poets from the previous two centuries. (OCD s.v. Meleager [2])

*The first European play*
Aeschylus' *Suppliants* (circa 491 B.C.) holds the distinction of being the first known play by any European author, Greek or otherwise. (Hadas 79)

*The first fabulist*
Although Aesop is most often associated with fables and fable writing, Quintilian (5.11) suggests that Hesiod was probably the first fabulist.

*The first female physician*
The Athenian woman Agnodice is considered the first female physician; since women were not permitted to study medicine in Athens, she disguised herself as a man in order to gain her medical training. Reputedly in part because of her initiative, Athenian law was revised to allow women to pursue medical careers, especially as midwives. (OCD s.v. Agnodice)

*The first grammarian to label nouns and verbs*
Plato was reportedly the first grammarian to describe and label nouns and verbs; the former he called *onoma*, the latter *rhema*. (Sandys 22)

*The first Greek grammaticus*
Antidorus of Cyme (circa 300 B.C.) is thought to have been the first Greek scholar to call himself *grammaticus*, "grammarian." He is credited with a treatise on Homer and Hesiod. (OCD s.v. Antidorus)

*The first Greek historian to recognize Roman achievement*
According to Hadas (228), Polybius was the first Greek writer on Roman affairs "to appreciate the greatness of Rome." However, the first Greek historian to provide substantial information about Roman history in his work was Timaeus of Tauromenium (Sicily; fl. early third century B.C.).

Timaeus was also associated with several other firsts: he was the first historian to evaluate his literary forebears, whether historians or not. His judgments were often so unkind that he became known by the epithet *Epitimaeus*, "Too much Timaeus," a name first conferred upon him by the third century B.C. writer Ister. His list of Olympic winners may have served as the impetus for the custom of numbering years by Olympiads. (OCD s.vv. Ister; Timaeus)

### The first Greek sculptor to work in Rome

The fourth century B.C. sculptor Polycles may have been the first prominent Greek sculptor to settle in Rome. (OCD s.v. Polycles)

### The first head librarian: Alexandria

The first head of the great library at Alexandria was Zenodotus of Ephesus (circa 325–234 B.C.). He assumed his duties around 285. He was the first scholar to produce what Sandys termed a "scientific edition of the *Iliad* and *Odyssey*" (p. 34), in the process becoming the first editor to divide the two epics into 24 books each.

### The first head-to-head competition between Sophocles and Aeschylus

The tragic playwrights Sophocles and Aeschylus first presented plays in competition with one another in 468 B.C. Sophocles triumphed, his first dramatic victory. According to Plutarch (*Life of Cimon* 8), this was also Sophocles' first competition, although modern scholars dispute this assertion. (CAH IV 120; OCD s.v. Sophocles)

### The first Homeric collator

The tyrant Pisistratus is said to have been the first to collect and organize the poems of Homer. (Sandys 2) However, in the Platonic(?) dialogue *Hipparchus*, the title character Hipparchus (Pisistratus' son) was credited with being the first to have performed this literary task.

### The first iambic poet

Archilochus was the first poet to employ iambic meter in his writing (OCD s.v. Archilochus). Ausonius (*Epistle* 25) states that a poorly attested poet named Iambus was the "first to link new rhythmic feet" in this style. (tr. Evelyn-White [LCL] 91)

### The first iron welder

The first craftsman to weld iron was reputedly the seventh century B.C. artisan Glaucus of Chios. Among other works, he crafted an iron stand for a silver bowl, which greatly impressed Herodotus. (Herodotus 1.25; OCD s.v. Glaucus [4])

*The first known military treatise*

The fourth century B.C. military writer Aeneas Tacticus compiled the first known handbook on military tactics: *Siegecraft.* (OCD s.v. Aeneas Tacticus)

*The first known use of metal struts in a building*

The ornate Propylaea, the gateway to the Acropolis in Athens, was constructed with iron-reinforced ceiling beams, the first time that such metal supports were used in a marble structure. (De Camp 87)

*The first known western Greek historian*

It is thought that Antiochus of Syracuse (fl. fifth century B.C.) was the first Greek historian from the western colonies (southern Italy, Sicily). He wrote a history of Sicily, and a treatise on city founding in southern Italy. (OCD s.v. Antiochus [10])

*The first line drawer*

According to Pliny the Elder (35.16), the first artist to produce line drawings was either Philocles of Egypt or Cleanthes of Corinth. The first artists to work extensively in the genre were Aridices of Corinth and Telephanes of Sicyon. The first to add color to line drawings was reputedly Ecphantus of Corinth.

*The first literary critic*

Dionysius of Halicarnassus, in his *Scripta Rhetorica*, was the first ancient author to employ standards of literary criticism to which modern critics also subscribe. (Hadas 235)

*The first literary fable*

Hesiod's anecdote about the hawk and the nightingale (*Works and Days* 202–212) is generally considered to be the earliest attested use of a fable in Greek literature. Demetrius of Phaleron (fl. fourth century B.C.) produced the first known anthology of Aesop's fables. (OCD s.v. Aesop)

*The first locks and keys*

Spartan craftsmen reportedly designed and fabricated the ancient world's first locks and keys. These craftsmen were also said to have provided Spartan soldiers with the first steel weapons. (Previously, metal weapons were made of iron or bronze.) (De Camp 99)

*The first "love" poet*

Apollonius of Rhodes was the first epic poet to give a central role to a romantic element in an epic poem: the love affair between Jason and Medea in his *Argonautica*. Apollonius was also the first epic poet to organize his material into separate chapters, or books. (The *Iliad* and *Odyssey*, for example, although obviously predating Apollonius, were not divided into books until long after Homer's time.) (OCD s.v. Apollonius)

### The first lunar scholar

The first man to attempt written explanations of various lunar phenomena, including eclipses, was Anaxagoras. His theories were not kindly received, and eventually he was imprisoned. (Plutarch *Life of Nicias* 23)

### The first medical illustrator

Anatomical drawings were first produced by Aristotle, to accompany and elucidate his writings on the organs of the human body. (OCD s.v. anatomy and physiology)

### The first name given to Homer

Originally, Homer was reputedly called Melesigenes, a reference to the Meles River in Smyrna. ([Author unknown] *Contest between Homer and Hesiod* 313)

### The first named poems

Hadas (56) suggests that the poems of Stesichorus were evidently the first ones to have received titles. He also states (55–56) that Stesichorus "was apparently the first ... to see the tragic implications in the passion of love."

### The first noted marble sculptors

The first sculptors to become famous for their marble images were Dipoenus and Scyllis, both early sixth century B.C. Cretans. (Pliny the Elder 35.153)

### The first nude depiction of Aphrodite

Praxiteles' (fifth century B.C. sculptor) statue of Aphrodite in the nude was reportedly the first depiction of Aphrodite — or any female figure — without clothing. (DCM s.v. Cnidus; Praxiteles)

### The first one to attend Lysistrata's meeting (and the first ones that should have attended)

Aristophanes' play *Lysistrata* opens with the title character (Lysistrata) impatiently complaining that no women had yet appeared at the special meeting she has organized. The first to arrive: her neighbor, Calonice. The first out-of-towners that would have been expected — the Acharnians, the ones living closest to Athens — were no-shows at the play's outset.

*The first outdoor class at the Lyceum*

According to Diogenes Laertius (7.185), Chrysippus was the first teacher at the Lyceum to lecture to a class out of doors.

*The first painter to realistically portray human emotions*

The fourth century B.C. painter Aristides of Thebes was the first to effectively capture in his paintings a range of human emotions and feelings. (Pliny the Elder 35.98)

*The first paroemiographer*

Paroemiography — the collecting of proverbs — began with Aristotle, in his book entitled *Paroimiai*. (OCD s.v. paroemiography)

*The first performance of a tragic play at the Dionysian Festival*

Sometime within the period from 535 to 533 B.C., the first tragic play was presented at the Dionysian festival in Athens. The author was Thespis, although his play does not survive. (OCD s.v. Thespis)

*The first pharmaceutical writer*

The first author to compose a systematic manual on drugs was the physician Mantias (circa 165–85 B.C.). He also wrote treatises on other medical topics, such as pathology. (OCD s.v. Mantias)

*The first philosopher to give credence to reason*

According to Plutarch (*Life of Pericles* 4), the philosopher Anaxagoras "was the first to enthrone in the universe not Chance [*tyche*] nor yet Necessity [*anagke*] as the source of its orderly arrangement, but Mind [*nous*] ... which distinguishes and sets apart ... the substances which have like elements." (tr. Perrin [LCL] 13)

*The first playwright to portray the torture of slaves*

The authors of *Suidas* state that Neophron of Sicyon "was the first to introduce paedagogi [slaves entrusted with the care of children] and the torture of slaves" into his tragic plays. (OCD [quoting *Suidas*] s.v. Neophron)

*The first political elegist*

The first Greek poet to create a political elegy was Callinus of Ephesus (fl. circa 700 B.C.). His only surviving fragment is evidently directed to the young men of Ephesus, to repel a foreign invader. (Harper's s.v. Callinus; Hadas 46)

*The first profitable poet*

The first Greek poet known to have earned substantial honoraria for his literary endeavors was Simonides, the sixth century epinicean poet. (Hadas 56)

*The first prose work on philosophy*

Anaximander of Miletus (circa 611–547 B.C.) was the first to write a prose work on philosophy, *On the Nature of Things*; this may also have been the first prose Greek literary work of any kind, although some regard the mythographer Pherecydes as the first Greek prose author; others (notably Pliny the Elder [5.112]) credit Cadmus with being the first. Anaximander also invented the sundial, and may have been the first to make a serious attempt at mapmaking. (Harper's s.v. Anaximander; Hadas 68; OCD s.v. Pherecydes)

*The first public dissections*

The first medical researcher to conduct public dissections of human bodies was the Alexandrian physician Herophilus (fl. early third century B.C.). He was also the first to correctly determine the function of nonsensory nerves, and the first to distinguish the roles of veins and arteries. Finally, he was also reportedly the first physician to instruct female students. (OCD s.v. anatomy and physiology)

*The first reference to silens*

The first reference to silens (wild, uncivilized woodland dwellers) in Greek literature may be found in the Homeric hymn to Venus. (OCD s.v. satyrs and silens)

*The first reference to Timon*

Timon, a well known Athenian misanthrope (later immortalized by Shakespeare), was first mentioned in a literary text by the comic playwright Aristophanes. (OCD s.v. Timon)

*The first responsibility of a choregus*

A *choregus* (financial backer of a play or plays) had numerous obligations; first and foremost, he was required to organize the chorus for the dramatic presentation which he was bankrolling. (OCD s.v. *choregoi*)

*The first rhapsodists in Athens*

The first rhapsodists (minstrels who specialized in recitations, especially of Homeric works) were introduced into Athens by Demetrius of Phalerum in the fourth century B.C. (Athenaeus 620B)

*The first rule in studying poetry*

*Polla pseudontai aoidoi*: "The poets [which includes playwrights] lie about many things." According to Plutarch (*Moralia* 16 A), this is the first truism which one must keep in mind when embarking upon a study of poetry. Sometimes poets lie intentionally, Plutarch claims, in order to embellish or enliven their plots; sometimes unintentionally, when they sincerely believe that the fiction which they write is actually the truth.

## The first scholar to study the history of lyric poetry

Glaucus of Rhegium (fl. circa 400 B.C.), author of a work entitled *On the Ancient Poets and Musicians*, is thought to have been the scholar who initiated critical studies of the history of lyric poetry. (OCD s.v. Glaucus [5])

## The first sculpted representation of Harmodius and Aristogiton

The first sculptor to fashion bronze images of Harmodius and Aristogiton, assassins of the tyrant Hipparchus (514 B.C.), was Antenor, an Athenian who flourished in the late sixth century B.C. (OCD s.v. Antenor [2])

## The first sculptor to see the big picture

According to Pliny the Elder (34.58), the fifth century B.C. sculptor Myron was *primus ... multiplicasse veritatem videur,* "the first [sculptor] who appears to have enlarged the scope of realism." (tr. Rackham Vol. IX [LCL] 171)

## The first sculptor to write about proportions

The Athenian sculptor Silanion (fl. fourth century B.C.) was the first sculptural portrait artist to write a treatise on proportions. It is thought that his statue of Plato provided a precedent for subsequent statues of philosophers: robed, seated, and striking a thoughtful pose. (OCD s.v. Silanion)

## The first skene painter

The painted backdrop in a Greek theater was called a skene; the first artist known to have been commissioned to produce a skene was Agatharcus of Samos (fl. fifth century B.C.). Agatharcus also wrote a book on the subject. Additionally, he was "the first painter to use perspective on a large scale ... probably in architectural backgrounds for plays." (OCD s.v. Agatharcus)

## The first Socratic disciple to charge for his teaching

Socrates' disciple Aristippus of Cyrene was reputedly the first member of the Socratic circle to charge listeners for the privilege of partaking of his philosophical lectures and teachings. (OCD s.v. Aristippus [1])

## The first sophist to claim the title

The first of the class of Greek sophists to call himself by that title was Protagoras of Abdera. (Harper's s.v. Protagoras; Hadas 72)

## The first structures on the Athenian Acropolis

Large-scale temples were first constructed on the Acropolis in the sixth century B.C. The first major building to be built under the leadership of Pericles and Phidias was the Parthenon; work began on this celebrated temple in 447. (OCD s.v. Athens [Acropolis])

### The first surviving work on meteorology

Aristotle's treatise *Meteorology* (subject matter: astronomical and geological phenomena; weather) is the earliest extant book on the subject. (OCD s.v. meteorology)

### The first systematizer of medicine

Although Hippocrates is sometimes regarded as the father of medicine, other physicians antedated him. Rather, he (and his associates) were the first to organize medical knowledge under logical rubrics and publish the data in systematized form. (Hadas 70)

### The first textual critic

Zenodotus, head of the library at Alexandria, is generally recognized as the originator of textual criticism. He was the first to edit the *Iliad* and the *Odyssey*, his chief claim to fame. (Hadas 198; Harper's s.v. Zenodotus)

### The first to annotate Plato

The first scholar to produce an annotated edition of one of Plato's works was Crantor of Soli in Cilicia (circa 335–275 B.C.); he composed a commentary on the *Timaeus*. (OCD s.v. Crantor)

### The first to beautify Athens

According to Plutarch (*Life of Cimon* 13), Cimon was the first Athenian leader to beautify the city with "places of public resort." He enhanced the attractiveness of these places by planting trees, constructing paths and providing water for drinking.

He also conceived the idea of the Long Walls: two parallel walls extending from Athens to its port city, Piraeus.

### The first to compile chronological lists of plays

Aristotle was apparently the first scholar to research and compile chronological lists of the titles of earlier Greek plays. (Sandys 13–14)

### The first to define logos (statement; assertion)

The philosopher Antisthenes, founder of the Cynic philosophical sect, was also the "first to define statement by saying that a statement is that which sets forth what a thing was or is." (Diogenes Laertius 6.3; tr. Hicks [LCL] 5)

*The first to design interdisciplinary studies*

The philosopher Speusippus (Plato's successor as head of the Academy) was the first to observe the commonalities in diverse fields of study, and the first to attempt to articulate these commonalities. (Diogenes Laertius 4.2)

*The first to hasten oratory's decline*

Although Quintilian (10.1) refers to Demetrius of Phalerum (fl. fourth century B.C.) as an eloquent and capable man, he also blames him for being "the first to set oratory on the downward path," apparently from the eminence which it had achieved through Demosthenes and the other Attic orators. (tr. Butler Vol. IV [LCL] 47)

*The first to mention color gradations in marble*

The fourth century B.C. comic playwright Menander (whom Pliny calls *diligentissimus luxuriae interpres*, "the incredibly exacting elucidator of luxury") was the first writer to mention color gradations and variations in marble. (Pliny the Elder 36.44)

*The first to play an 11-string lyre*

The Athenian Stratonicus (fourth century B.C.) was the first to play an 11-string lyre, thus enabling him to produce many notes and sounds. He was also the first to accept and train students in the art of harmonics, and the first "to compile a table of musical intervals." (Athenaeus 352C; tr. Gulick Vol. IV [LCL] 97; OCD s.v. Stratonicus)

*The first to publicize Homeric epic*

According to Plutarch (*Life of Lycurgus* 4), Lycurgus of Sparta was the first man to make Homeric epic widely known, although Plutarch notes that Homer's work had been familiar to peoples living in Asia Minor prior to the Lycurgan era.

*The first to record Socrates' words*

An Athenian shoemaker named Simon was reportedly the first to cast Socrates' philosophical musings in dialogue form, although some modern authorities consider Simon to have been a fictitious character. (OCD s.v. Simon)

*The first to suspend judgment*

The philosopher Arcesilaus (circa 318–242 B.C.) was said by Diogenes Laertius (4.28, 32) to have been the first to delay forming opinions or making judgments in philosophical discussions. His reluctance to take positions obviated whatever literary career may have lain open to him; Diogenes relates that he never wrote a book, an oddity in an era when many of his like-minded colleagues authored dozens of treatises and essays.

### The first to teach rhetoric

Diogenes Laertius (2.20) asserts that Socrates and Aeschines were the first rhetoric teachers.

### The first to use accents in writing Greek

Aristophanes of Byzantium is generally thought to have been the first author to use accent marks in written Greek. He was also the first to collate and organize the poems of Pindar. (OCD s.v. Aristophanes [2])

### The first to write biographies of philosophers

Aristoxenus of Tarentum (born between 375 and 360 B.C.) was the first to compose biographies of philosophers; included were entries on Plato, Socrates and Pythagoras. (OCD svv. Aristoxenus; philosophy, history of)

### The first to write dialogues

Diogenes Laertius (3.48) states that Plato was the first to write dialogues, although he notes that various other sources credit either Zeno the Eleatic or Alexamenus of Styra (or Teos) with this distinction.

### The first to write on geometric topics

Hippocrates of Chios (fl. fifth century B.C.) is said to have been the first Greek to author a treatise on the basics of geometry; his work may have been a source for the more famous book on the subject, Euclid's *Elements*. (OCD s.v. Hippocrates [3])

### The first travel manual

Scylax of Caryanda is thought to have written the first travelogue (*periplous*), at the behest of King Darius I. Scylax's book describes a voyage down the Indus River, to the isthmus of Suez. (OCD s.vv. *periplous*; Scylax)

### The first well-attested harbor

The first well-known harbor in the classical world was the one constructed at Samos, in the sixth century B.C., under the supervision of the celebrated tyrant Polycrates. (Herodotus 3.60; OCD s.v. harbours)

### The first words spoken to Hesiod by the Muses

In his *Theogony* (26–28), Hesiod asserts that the Muses, his literary mentors, first spoke these words to him:

> Shepherds of the wilderness,
> wretched things of shame, mere bellies,
> we know how to speak many false things,
> as though they were true; but we know,
> when we will, to utter true things.
> (tr. Evelyn-White
> [LCL] 81)

Hesiod notes in the same passage (at line 44) that the first topic of the Muses' revelation to him concerned the first gods.

### The first writer of mimes

The Syracusan writer Sophron is considered to have been the first to give form to the mime as a literary genre. Plato held him in high regard; according to Diogenes Laertius (3.18), Plato was the first to introduce Sophron's mimes in Athens. (Diogenes Laertius loc. cit.; OCD s.v. Sophron)

### The first writer of off-color poetry

According to Strabo (14.1), Sotades of Magnesia (fl. third century B.C.) was the first to write cineadic poetry, verses on obscene themes.

### Golden firsts

Gorgias of Leontini erected the first golden statue of a person — the orator himself— in the fifth century B.C. Apollo's temple in Delphi housed the work. The first golden statue of a deity was said to have been produced in Anaitica (modern Near East; the source for this information, Pliny the Elder, does not provide an approximate date of the deity's name).

The latter statue was brought to Rome around 36 B.C., among the war spoils won from the Parthians by Mark Antony. Rumor had it that the first man to dishonor the Anaitican deity (by seizing the statue) would be blinded, paralyzed, and then killed. Once, when Augustus was dining as the guest of a veteran soldier of the Parthian expedition, he asked his host about the rumor. The soldier laughed and told Augustus that they were eating on a place setting crafted from the statue, that he himself was the temple robber, and that he owed his entire fortune to his possession of the statute. (Pliny the Elder 33.82–83)

### The grammatical innovations of Aristophanes of Byzantium

Aristophanes of Byzantium, the fourth head of the library at Alexandria, was credited with a number of innovations. He reputedly invented the following marks of punctuation: hyphen; comma; colon; period. He was the first to employ accent marks (grave, acute, circumflex). He also devised a number of symbols for use in editing texts. (Sandys 38)

### Hesiod's first call to write poetry

The Muses first enjoined Hesiod to write poetry while he was tending his flocks on Mount Helicon. He says that he later dedicated a tripod to them at that place; he had won the tripod in a celebrated poetry contest in Chalcis. (Hesiod *Works and Days* 657–659)

### Pausias' firsts

The fourth century B.C. painter Pausias is credited with two innovations: He was the first to decorate ceiling coffers with paintings, and the first to effectively use the encaustic technique of painting (in which pigments are mixed with melted beeswax.) (OCD s.v. Pausias)

### Plutarch's first motivation for writing biographies

Plutarch confesses (*Life of Timoleon* 1) that while he first embarked upon writing biographies for the edification of others, he eventually continued doing so primarily for his own benefit.

### Polygnotus' firsts

The fifth century B.C. painter Polygnotus of Thasos was credited by Pliny with several artistic firsts:

1. He was the first to depict women clothed in transparent drapery, and the first to portray them with multicolored headwear.
2. He was the first to paint subjects with open mouths, revealing teeth. He was also, therefore, the first to bestow upon them a kind of facial realism not achieved by his predecessors. (Pliny the Elder 35.58)

Quintilian (12.10) adds that Polygnotus, along with his father Aglaophon, were the *primi clari pictores*, "first celebrated painters."

### Some firsts in the Alexandrian literary competitions

Ptolemy II was instrumental in founding the great library at Alexandria. To commemorate the glorious occasion, he established competitions in athletics and writing. Some firsts in the writing competitions:

The first contest was among poets. The audience was to decide the first-prize winner, basing its verdict on the degree to which each poet's work was pleasing to it. The seven judges of the contestants were expected to follow popular opinion.

At the conclusion of the contest, six of the seven judges voted as expected.

However, the seventh judge, Aristophanes of Byzantium, preferred the *least* popular poet, arguing that he should be given the first prize. His rationale: because of his extensive and detailed knowledge of literature, he immediately recognized that the other contestants had all plagiarized their entries; therefore, the prize ought to be conferred upon the author of the only original work.

Ptolemy was so impressed by Aristophanes' arguments and his erudition that he exiled the literary thieves and placed Aristophanes in charge of the library. (Vitruvius 7 [preface])

### Terpander's firsts

Terpander of Antissa (fl. seventh century B.C.) founded and prevailed in the first citharodic (lyre) contest, around 676 B.C. He was also the inventor of the seven-stringed lyre. (OCD s.v. Terpander)

## Roman

### Acrostics formed from the first letter of lines

Acrostics, words or phrases "formed from the initial letters of a number of consecutive lines of verse" (OCD s.v. acrostics), occur occasionally in Greek and Latin literature. Some Latin examples:

1. Cicero notes (although without specific quotations) that certain consecutive lines of Quintus Ennius' poems begin with words containing the initial letters q, q, e and f, for *quae Quintus Ennius fecit*, "things which Quintus Ennius created." He also remarks that in the prophetic Sibylline books, "each prophecy is embellished with an acrostic, so that the initial letters of each line give the subject of that particular prophecy." (Cicero *On Divination* 2.111–112; tr. Falconer [LCL] 497)

2. Some commentators see a "reverse acrostic" in the alternating lines of Vergil's *Georgic* 1.429–433, where line 429 begins with *Maxumus*, 431 with *ventus*, 433 with *pura*. The two initial letters of each of those words duplicate the first two letters of Vergil's three names: *Pu*blius *Ve*rgilius *Ma*ro.

3. In the seventh book of Vergil's *Aeneid* (lines 601ff.) the poet describes the manner in which the god of war is roused to arms. The first four lines of the account (601–604) begin with the words *mos, Albanae, Roma, sive*; the initial letters of the four words from the god's name: Mars.

4. Synopses of Plautus' plays typically form acrostics. An example, from his play *Aulularia* (*Pot of Gold*, where "u" and "v" are interchangeable):

> *A*ulam repertam auri plenam Euclio
> *V*i summa servat, miseris adfectus modis.
> *L*yconides istius vitiat filiam.
> *V*olt hanc Megadorus indotatam ducere,
> *L*ubensque ut faciat dat coquos cum obsonio.
> *A*uro formidat Euclio, abstrudit foris.
> *R*e omni inspecta compressoris servolus
> *I*d surpit. Illic Euclioni rem refert.
> *A*b eo donatur auro, uxore et filio.

Euclio, on finding a pot full of gold, is dreadfully worried, and watches over it with the greatest vigilance. Lyconides wrongs his daughter. This girl, undowered though she is, Megadorus wishes to marry, and he cheerfully supplies cooks and provisions for the wedding feast. Anxious about his gold, Euclio hides it outside the house. Everything he does having been witnessed, a rascally servant of the girl's assailant steals it. His master informs Euclio of it, and receives from him gold, wife, and son. (tr. Nixon Vol. I [LCL] 233)

### Cicero's first prosecution

Throughout his career as an attorney, Cicero preferred to defend rather than prosecute. His first well-documented prosecution occurred in the summer of 70 B.C., against Gaius Verres, the corrupt ex-governor of Sicily. (OCD s.v. Cicero)

### The earliest known cento

The writing of centos (poems comprised of excerpts from well-known, existing poems) became popular in Roman imperial times. The earliest known cento poem is *Medea*, thought to have been authored by Hosidius Geta (fl. second century A.D.) (OCD s.v. cento [Latin])

### The first accomplished wall painter

The first century A.D. mural artist Spurius Tadius was the first to decorate the walls of homes with various kinds of pastoral scenes, and also vignettes from daily life: people fishing, hunting, riding, sailing, walking. (Pliny the Elder 35.116)

### The first advantage of a short book

At the beginning of his second book of poems (2.1), Martial lists three advantages of a short book. The first of these: it does not waste much paper. (The other two: a secretary can transcribe it quickly; and, when read aloud, the book will bore an audience for only a short time.)

*A first and only in theater construction*

In 52 B.C., Gaius Scribonius Curio initiated and oversaw the construction of a truly unique style of theater, or more accurately, paired theaters: they faced in opposite directions and were built on pivots. When not facing each other, they were used for dramatic presentations; on other occasions, they could be rotated toward one another, to form an amphitheater for gladiatorial shows. (Pliny the Elder 36.117)

*The first annalist*

Quintus Ennius (239–169 B.C.) was the first Roman historian to refer to his writings as *Annales, Annals* (year-by-year accounts). (OCD s.vv. annalists; annals)

*The first annals*

The *tabulae pontificum*—daily records of pontifical actions—were the first true Roman annals; *tabulae* became well documented by the fourth century B.C., and were systematized by about 300. (OCD s.v. annals, annalists)

*The first author to write about the medicinal uses of plants*

Cato the Elder was the first Roman author who dealt with the healing properties of plants. The first author to treat the subject in detail was Gaius Valgius, who flourished in the time of Augustus, and who dedicated his book to that emperor. (Pliny the Elder 25.4)

*The first book-form reports to the Senate*

When military commanders prepared written reports for the Senate, they customarily wrote them on separate sheets of paper, with no columns or margins. Julius Caesar was reportedly the first commander to make his reports in either scroll or codex form, with columns and margins carefully observed. (Suetonius *Life of Julius Caesar* 56, with Rolfe's comment [LCL] 78)

*The first bronze statue of a deity*

A bronze statue of the goddess Ceres, the first of its kind in Rome, was set up around 485 B.C.; it was financed from the proceeds of the confiscated estate of Spurius Cassius, executed because of his designs on a kingship. (Pliny the Elder 34.15)

*The first Corinthian-style structure in Rome*

The first structure in Rome utilizing Corinthian columns was the Porticus Octavia (168 B.C.). (Granger *Vitruvius* Vol. I. [LCL] 202)

*The first critical edition of Vergil*

The first critical edition of Vergil's works was prepared by Marcus Valerius

Probus, in the mid–first century A.D. Probus also produced the first edition of Horace's poems. (Sandys 58)

### The first datable amphitheater

The earliest datable amphitheater was located in Pompeii; approximate date of construction was 80 B.C. (OCD s.v. amphitheater)

### The first deputy water commissioner

When private citizens wished to obtain water from the aqueducts, they were required to procure the emperor's permission; the emperor then delegated the matter to the water commissioner. According to Frontinus (*Aqueducts* 105), Tiberius was apparently the first emperor to appoint a deputy water commissioner to assist in the processing of these water rights permissions.

### The first distinction between military and commercial harbors

In the earliest days of Greek and Roman seafaring, harbors served both military and commercial ventures. However, under the Roman empire, separate harbors began to be constructed for the first time. (OCD s.v. harbors)

### The first duty of a teacher

Quintilian (1.3) asserts that a teacher's first duty is to assess the talent and aptitude of his students.

### The first equestrian to teach in Rome

A certain Rubellius Blandus was the first Roman equestrian to teach in Rome; he offered instruction in rhetoric and oratory. Prior to his time, such teaching was the responsibility of freedmen. (Seneca *Controversies* 2 [preface])

### The first extant book on Latin grammar

Marcus Terentius Varro's *De Lingua Latina* (*On the Latin Language*) stands as the earliest extant work on the subject. Varro was also the first to author a work in Latin on the nine liberal arts, which he identified as grammar, logic, rhetoric, geometry, arithmetic, astronomy, music, medicine and architecture. (Sandys 55)

### The first extant work on oratory

The treatise entitled *Rhetorica ad Herennium*—sometimes ascribed to Cicero—is the oldest extant Latin work on oratory. Throughout antiquity and the early Middle Ages, its authorship was universally attributed to Cicero; the first to question the work's authorship was the fifteenth century scholar Lorenzo Valla. (Caplan [LCL] vii, ix)

*The first extension of the Roman forum*

By the first century B.C., it became apparent that the Roman forum no longer was large enough to serve the needs of a growing and expanding civilization. So Julius Caesar undertook the first enlargement of the forum. The real estate required for this expansion cost more than 100,000,000 sesterces, which Caesar provided from war spoils. (Suetonius *Life of Julius Caesar* 26)

*The first Fabius Pictor*

Gaius Fabius, grandfather of the historian Quintus Fabius Pictor, was the first member of the family to have the cognomen Pictor, "Painter." He earned the title by virtue of paintings he made for the Temple of Salus around 304 B.C. (Pliny the Elder 35.19)

*The first fabulae trabeatae*

Stage plays portraying Roman life (*fabulae togatae*) and their Greek antecedents (*fabulae palliatae*) were long popular in Rome. The librarian/grammarian Gaius Melissus (fl. during the reign of Augustus) invented a third installment in the genre: the *fabula trabeata*. This was a form of the *togata* in which the characters were represented as Roman knights, wearing togas marked by *trabeae*, purple stripes. (Suetonius *On Grammarians* 21; Rolfe Vol. II [LCL] 426–427)

*The first famous teacher*

According to Suetonius (*On Grammarians* 5), the first teacher to gain fame and recognition in Rome was a certain Saevius Nicanor. Saevius was also noted for his literary attainments, although none of his work is extant.

*The first foreign painting displayed in Rome*

The first foreign painting displayed on public property in Rome was a portrait of Dionysus, by Aristides. This portrait was hung in the Temple of Ceres, by the consul Lucius Mummius, about 146 B.C. (Pliny the Elder 35.24)

*The first freedman to write history*

Suetonius (*On Rhetoricians* 3), quoting Cornelius Nepos' opinion, states that a certain Lucius Voltacilius Plotus (fl. first century B.C.) was the first Roman freedman to write history, a task which only men of more noble birth had aspired to prior to that time. Plotus was a teacher of Pompey the Great, and wrote a multivolume account of Pompey's accomplishments, as well as those of Pompey's father.

*The first heated swimming pool*

The first heated swimming pool in Rome was constructed by Maecenas. (Balsdon 27)

*The first large scale public bath*
The first *thermae* (large, public bathing establishment) was built under the auspices of Marcus Vipsanius Agrippa, in the Campus Martius. (Balsdon 27)

*The first Latin lexicon*
The first Latin lexicon — *De Verborum Significatu* (*On the Meaning of Words*) — was written by Verrius Flaccus (fl. late first century B.C.); fragments of the treatise survive. (Sandys 60)

*The first Latin lyric poet*
Horace was the (self-proclaimed) first Latin lyric poet. (OCD s.v. lyric poetry)

*The first left-handed artist*
According to Pliny the Elder (35.20), a first century A.D. Roman knight named Turpilius was the first known left-handed artist.

*The first literary historians*
Cicero (*Orator* 39, quoting Theophrastus) records that Herodotus and Thucydides were the first historians to elevate written history into a more literary and ornate style.

*The first "live" Roman personality*
Appius Claudius Caecus (censor 312 B.C.; consul 307 and 296; praetor 295) has been described as "the first live personality in Roman history" (OCD s.v. Claudius Caecus, Appius). During his censorship, he oversaw the construction of the first Roman aqueduct, the Aqua Appia.

*The first marble temple*
According to Velleius Paterculus (1.11), the first Roman to construct a temple of marble was Quintus Caecilius Metellus Macedonicus, apparently in the middle of the second century B.C.

*The first maturity of spoken Latin*
Cicero dates the mature emergence of spoken Latin to a speech given by his oratorical idol, Lucius Licinius Crassus, in 106 B.C.; the speech concerned the *Lex Servilia* (regarding jury composition). Cicero terms the occasion the *prima maturitas*, "first maturity" of spoken Latin. (*Brutus* 161)

*The first non–Roman to write accurately about Rome*
Theophrastus of Eresus (circa 372–286 B.C.), a friend and colleague of

Aristotle, was identified by Pliny the Elder (3.57) as the first non–Roman who wrote carefully and accurately about the Romans.

### The first "nosey" critic

In an interestingly turned phrase in the introduction to his *Natural History*, Pliny the Elder refers to the satirist Gaius Lucilius as the one *qui primus condidit stili nasum*, "the originator of critical sniffing" (tr. Rackham), literally, the one "who first founded the nose of the stilus." (Pliny the Elder *Preface* 7; Rackham Vol. I [LCL] 6)

### The first noted rhetoric instructor

Marcus Porcius Latro (died circa A.D. 4) was the first rhetorician to become famous for his ability to teach the rhetorical art. However, he apparently fell into the category of "those who can, do; those who can't, teach": when he was requested to declaim in the (open air) forum, he begged that the case be heard in a roofed hall, à la a classroom, the only kind of place where he felt comfortable. (Quintilian 10.5)

### The first obelisks in Rome

The first two obelisks seen in Rome were brought there from Egypt by Augustus; the task was undertaken by specially constructed transport ships. The ship which conveyed the first of the obelisks to Rome was later permanently moored in Puteoli, as a kind of floating tourist attraction.

The Egyptians were the first people to construct obelisks; the first king to order the carving of an obelisk was Mesphres. (Pliny the Elder 36.64, 70)

### The first Pantheon

The Pantheon, as seen today, is the second century A.D. reconstruction of the original structure; the first Pantheon was built under the supervision of Marcus Vipsanius Agrippa, in 27–25 B.C. (OCD s.v. Pantheon)

### The first pantomimic performers in Rome

Pylades of Cilicia and Bathyllus of Alexandria introduced pantomimes (dramatic presentations accompanied by music, but with no speaking) in Rome in 22 B.C. (OCD s.v. pantomime)

### The first poet to discuss grammatical matters

Gaius Lucilius was the first poet who touched upon grammatical matters in his poetry. (Duff 179)

### The first poetry written by a Roman woman

The earliest extant poetry of a *docta puella*, "learned young woman," comes from the pen of the first century B.C. writer Sulpicia (daughter of the noted jurist and statesman Servius Sulpicius Rufus). Only 40 lines of her work survive, however. (OCD s.v. Sulpicia)

### The first public display of a painting in Rome

Manius Valerius Maximus Messalla first publicly displayed a painting in Rome, in 264 B.C. It depicted a battle in Sicily in which the Romans, under Messalla's command, had defeated the Carthaginians. (Pliny the Elder 35.22)

### The first reading of Terence's first play

The playwright Terence first recited his first play (*Andria*) to Caecilius Statius, while the latter was in the midst of his evening meal. Caecilius was so impressed by what he heard that he invited Terence to join him at the table. (Suetonius *Life of Terence* 2)

### The first representation of Jupiter in gold

According to Martial (11.4), a golden statue of Jupiter was first fashioned during the reign of Nerva. (Ker Vol. II [LCL] 239)

### The first rhetorical writer

Quintilian (3.1) indicates that Marcus Porcius Cato the Elder was probably the first Roman to write about rhetoric and oratory.

### The first Roman aqueduct

Rome's first major aqueduct was the Aqua Marcia, constructed in 144 B.C., under the supervision of the praetor Quintus Marcius Rex, for whom it was named. The Aqua Marcia was the first aqueduct to incorporate the prominent style of arches which became something of a trademark in later aqueducts. (OCD s.vv. aqueducts; Marcius Rex [1], Quintus)

### The first Roman scholar

Lucius Aelius, called "the first important Roman scholar" (OCD s.v. Aelius, Lucius), was born around 150 B.C. He authored treatises on Roman literature, law, philosophy, and drama, and also wrote speeches for Roman orators.

### The first Roman to attempt a universal history

According to Catullus, Cornelius Nepos' *Chronica* was the first foray by a Roman author into the writing of a universal history.

### The first Roman to open a school with salaried teachers

According to Plutarch (*Moralia* 277D; 278E), the third century B.C. freedman Spurius Carvilius founded the first school in which the teachers were paid a salary. This Carvilius reportedly also introduced the letter "q" into the Roman alphabet. He was the freedman of Spurius Carvilius Maximus (consul in 235), the first Roman to divorce his wife. (See also OCD s.v. Carvilius [1 and 2])

*The first Roman to write extensively on pharmacology*
Although Cato the Elder and Gaius Valgius both mentioned drugs and drug therapy in their writings, the first Roman to treat the subject in detail was Pompeius Lenaeus, a learned freedman of Pompey the Great. (Pliny the Elder 25.5)

*(One of ) the first Roman travelers*
One of the first Romans to travel in Asia Minor was the noted tragedian Lucius Accius (circa 170–90 B.C.). Accius was also the first critic to identify as spurious certain plays thought to have been authored by Plautus. (Sandys 54)

*The first rule of historical writing*
The first rule which must be followed by a historian: to be truthful. (Cicero *On the Orator* 2.62)

*The first salary for Latin and Greek rhetoric teachers*
According to Suetonius (*Life of Vespasian* 18), the emperor Vespasian initiated regular salaries for instructors of Latin and Greek rhetoric. Suetonius provides a salary figure of 100,000 sesterces, but he does not indicate the frequency with which that sum was to be paid.

*The first satirist*
Gaius Lucilius was the first practitioner of that uniquely Roman literary genre, satire. (Quintilian 10.1; in 10.1 may also be found Quintilian's well-known statement that the Romans invented satire: *Satira ... tota nostra est,* "Satire is completely ours.")

*The first scholar to present public lectures on the poets*
According to Suetonius (*On Grammarians* 16), Quintus Caecilius Epirota (fl. late first century B.C.) was the first man to read and interpret the poetry of Vergil and others in public settings. He also reportedly initiated the practice of holding impromptu scholarly discussions in Latin. Epirota was a freedman of Atticus, Cicero's celebrated correspondent.

*The first sculptor to portray certain anatomical features carefully*
According to Pliny the Elder (34.59), the sculptor Pythagoras of Rhegium

was the first to pay close attention to anatomically accurate depictions of muscles, veins, and hair in his artistry. Pliny notes that Pythagoras' statue of a lame man was so realistic that people often felt pain in their own legs while viewing it.

### The first source of marble

Pliny the Elder (36.46) expresses the opinion that Chios was the first place from which the Romans acquired quarried marble. Chian marble was evidently highly prized because of its gradations and varieties of colors.

### The first task in the Art of Love

In his poem *Ars Amatoria* (*Art of Love*), Ovid suggested that the first step in the process was (not surprisingly!) to find someone to love.

### The first term for grammarians

When grammarians began teaching and lecturing in Rome, they were initially called *litterati*, "lettered-men." Later, the Greek term *grammatici* became the one more commonly applied to them. (Suetonius *On Grammarians* 4)

### The first to aid in the Capitol cleanup

Early in his reign, the emperor Vespasian initiated some major urban renewal projects in Rome. Preliminary to the implementation of these plans was a general cleanup of the downtrodden central city. To show his enthusiasm for the project, he involved himself personally, by being the first person to haul away a basketful of rubble. (Suetonius *Life of Vespasian* 8)

### The first to apply Hellenistic methods to source material

According to the OCD (s.v. Gellius [2]), Gnaeus Gellius was the first annalist to use "Hellenistic methods in elaborating source material."

### The first to bridge the Gulf of Baiae

Caligula's feat of bridging the Gulf of Baiae — a distance of about three miles — was unprecedented. He accomplished this by ordering merchant ships to be lashed together, à la Xerxes' famous bridging of the Hellespont. His motives were varied; some thought that he was attempting to outdo Xerxes, while others believed that he was trying to intimidate the British and the Germans, against whom he had planned military excursions. Still others thought that he did this in response to an astrological pronouncement that he would have no more chance of gaining the emperorship than of riding a horse over the Gulf of Baiae. He discredited the prediction by riding a horse, and later driving a chariot, across the bridge. (Suetonius *Life of Caligula* 19)

*The first to teach grammar in Rome*

Crates of Mallos came to Rome in 169 B.C.; once there, he had the unfortunate experience of falling into an open sewer and fracturing his leg. During his recuperation, he taught his many visitors the principles of grammar and literary criticism, and served as a sort of exemplar for his successors. (Suetonius *On Grammarians* 2)

*The first to translate Greek technical terms into Latin*

According to Plutarch (*Life of Cicero* 40), Cicero was reputedly the first Roman to translate Greek scientific and philosophical technical terms into Latin.

*The first to wear a sardonyx ring*

The first Roman to wear a sardonyx ring was Scipio Africanus; according to Pliny the Elder (37.85), Africanus' digital display lent a certain credibility and prestige to rings set with this gemstone.

*The first to write about the phoenix*

The first Roman author to write about the mythical phoenix was Marcus Manilius (fl. first century A.D.). Pliny the Elder (10.3–5) states that the self-taught Manilius provided not only the first, but also the most detailed description of this miraculous bird.

*The first to write scripts for farces*

Farcical plays—*Atellanae*—originally depended heavily on improvisation. The first author to provide full scripts (instead of merely plot outlines) is generally thought to have been Lucius Pomponius Bononiensis. (Harper's s.v. Pomponius [1]; Rose 148)

*The first treatise exclusively on grammar*

The first treatise whose emphasis was wholly on Latin grammar was the *Ars Grammatica*, authored by the first century A.D. scholar Quintus Remmius Palaemon. He was also the first to identify and label four declensions for Latin nouns. Palaemon's influence was extended to one of his most noteworthy students, the grammarian Quintilian. (Sandys 60–61)

*The first use of marble and gilding in the circus*

The starting gates (*carceres*) and turning posts (*metae*) of the Circus Maximus were traditionally made of tufa and wood, respectively. The emperor Claudius was the first to replace these materials with more ornate forms: marble for the *carceres*, and gilding for the *metae*. (Suetonius *Life of Claudius* 21)

### The first use of marble veneering

Although marble veneering became quite popular in Roman construction, its first use — as far as Pliny was able to determine — was in Halicarnassus (modern southwestern Turkey), on the palace of Mausolus (fourth century B.C.). (Pliny the Elder 36.47)

### The first water commissioner

The first Roman official to hold the post of water commissioner (*curator aquarum*) on a permanent basis was Marcus Vipsanius Agrippa. He was appointed in 33 B.C. (Frontinus *Aqueducts of Rome* 2.98)

### The firsts of Quintus Caecilius Epirota

Quintus Caecilius Epirota (a freedman of Atticus, Cicero's well-known confidant) was credited with two literary firsts: he was the first to conduct unscripted discussions in Latin, presumably on literary topics; he initiated the practice of reading aloud the works of Vergil and other contemporary poets, presumably in a pedagogical context. (Suetonius *On Grammarians* 16)

### The inventor of shorthand

A system of shorthand writing was evidently unknown to the Greeks. The Roman inventor, and therefore first practitioner, of the art was reportedly Tiro, Cicero's secretary. Plutarch asserts that the first oration to be recorded in (Tironian?) shorthand was Cato the Younger's speech to the Roman Senate in 63 B.C., in the debate over capital punishment for the Catilinarian conspirators. (Plutarch *Life of Cato the Younger* 23; OCD s.v. tachography)

### Martial's first reason for writer's block

After having lived in Rome for some 34 years, Martial moved back to his native Spain in A.D. 98. Once there, however, he discovered that he missed the hustle and bustle of big city life, and that it was difficult to find the inspiration to write in bucolic Spain. This, at least, is the first reason he provides for his *trienni desidia,* "lazy three years," during which he apparently wrote little. (Martial 12 [introductory poem]; OCD s.v. Martial)

### The poet closer to first than to third

Quintilian (10.85) relates a story about a question he put to one of his teachers, Domitius Afer, namely, which poet came closest to Homer. Afer replied that, although Homer was universally regarded as history's best poet, Vergil was a very close second, much closer to first (Homer) than to third (all other poets).

*References to the first book in the second book*
Martial concludes Book II of his poetry with this epigram:

> "Where's the first book," you say, "if that is the second?"
> What's for me to do if my first book is too shy?
> Yet if *you*, Regulus, prefer that this should
> become the first, you can take one "I" from its title.
>
> (tr. Ker [LCL] 161)

*A temple precedent*
When the citizens of Tarraco (northeastern Spain) successfully petitioned Tiberius to allow them to construct a temple in honor of Augustus, it marked the first time that such a structure had been built in a province. (Tacitus *Annals* 1.78)

*Two supremely alliterative lines of poetry*
In the treatise *To Herennius* (sometimes ascribed to Cicero), the author quotes from plays by Ennius two lines which display inordinate repetition of words with the same first consonant: *O Tite, tute, Tati, tibi tanta, tyranne, tulisti* ("Thyself to thyself, Titus Tatius the tyrant, thou tookest those terrible troubles." [tr. Warmington (LCL) 37]), and, *Quoiquam quicquam quemquam, quemque quisque conveniat, neget* ("Let anyone deny anyone anything, whoever meets whomever." [tr. Warmington (LCL) 381])

*Vergil's first poem*
Vergil wrote his first poem, a two-line couplet, as a boy. It concerned the stoning to death of a teacher named Ballista, for his propensity for robbery. The poem: "Under this mountain of rocks is covered the buried Ballista. Night or day, traveler, your journey is now safe." (Suetonius *Lives of Illustrious Men: Vergil* 17)

*First speakers in dialogues, plays and poems*

| Title | Author | First character to speak |
|---|---|---|
| *Acharnians* | Aristophanes | Dicaeopolis |
| *Aeneid* | Vergil | Juno |
| *Affairs of the Heart* | Lucian(?) | Lycinus |
| *Agamemnon* | Aeschylus | guard |
| *Agamemnon* | Seneca | ghost of Thyestes |
| *Alcestis* | Euripides | Apollo |
| *Alcibiades I* | Plato | Socrates |
| *Alcibiades II* | uncertain | Socrates |
| *Amphitryon* | Plautus | Sosia |
| *Andromache* | Euripides | Andromache |

| *Title* | *Author* | *First character to speak* |
|---|---|---|
| *Assembly of the Gods* | Lucian | Zeus |
| *Bacchantes* | Euripides | Dionysus |
| *Birds* | Aristophanes | Euelpides |
| *Bragging Soldier* | Plautus | Pyrgopolynices |
| *Brothers* | Terence | Micio |
| *Captives* | Plautus | Ergasilus |
| *Casina* | Plautus | Olympio |
| *Charidemus* | Lucian(?) | Hermippus |
| *Charmides* | Plato | Socrates |
| *Children of Hercules* | Euripides | Iolaus |
| *Cistellaria* | Plautus | Selenium |
| *Clitophon* | uncertain | Socrates |
| *Clouds* | Aristophanes | Strepsiades |
| *Comedy of Asses* | Plautus | Libanus |
| *Cratylus* | Plato | Hermogenes |
| *Critias* | Plato | Timaeus |
| *Curculio* | Plautus | Palinurus |
| *Cyclops* | Euripides | Silenus |
| *Cynic* | Lucian(?) | Lycinus |
| *Dialogues of the Courtesans* | Lucian | Glycera |
| *Dialogues of the Dead* | Lucian | Diogenes |
| *Dialogues of the Gods* | Lucian | Ares |
| *Dialogues of the Sea Gods* | Lucian | Doris |
| *Double Indictment* | Lucian | Zeus |
| *Ecclesiazusae* | Aristophanes | Praxagora |
| *Electra* | Euripides | peasant |
| *Epidicus* | Plautus | Epidicus |
| *Epinomis* | uncertain | Clinias |
| *Eumenides* | Aeschylus | prophetess |
| *The Eunuch* | Lucian | Pamphilus |
| *The Eunuch* | Terence | Phaedria |
| *Euthydemus* | Plato | Crito |
| *The Fisherman* | Lucian | Socrates |
| *Frogs* | Aristophanes | Xanthias |
| *Gorgias* | Plato | Callicles |
| *Gout* | Lucian | gouty man |
| *Greater Hippias* | uncertain | Socrates |
| *Halcyon* | Lucian(?) | Chaerephon |
| *Haunted House* | Plautus | Grumio |
| *Hecuba* | Euripides | Polydorus |
| *Helen* | Euripides | Helen |
| *Hercules Oetaeus* | Seneca | Hercules |
| *Hermotimus* | Lucian | Lycinus |
| *Hipparchus* | uncertain | Socrates |
| *Hippolytus* | Euripides | Aphrodite |
| *Icaromenippus* | Lucian | Menippus |
| *Iliad* | Homer | Chryses |
| *Iphigenia at Aulis* | Euripides | Agamemnon |

| Title | Author | First character to speak |
|---|---|---|
| *Iphigenia in Taurus* | Euripides | Iphigenia |
| *Ion* | Euripides | Hermes |
| *Ion* | Plato | Socrates |
| *Judgment of the Goddesses* | Lucian | Zeus |
| *On Kingship* | Plato | Socrates |
| *Knights* | Aristophanes | Demosthenes |
| *Laches* | Plato | Lysimachus |
| *Laws* | Plato | Athenian stranger |
| *Lesser Hippias* | uncertain | Eudicus |
| *Lexiphanes* | Lucian | Lycinus |
| *Libation Bearers* | Aeschylus | Orestes |
| *Little Carthaginian* | Plautus | Agorastocles |
| *Lysis* | Plato | Socrates |
| *Lysistrata* | Aristophanes | Lysistrata |
| *Madness of Hercules* | Euripides | Amphitryon |
| *Medea* | Euripides | nurse |
| *Menaechmi Twins* | Plautus | Peniculus |
| *Menexenus* | Plato | Socrates |
| *Meno* | Plato | Meno |
| *Merchant* | Plautus | Charinus |
| *Minos* | uncertain | Socrates |
| *Mother-in-Law* | Terence | Philotis |
| *Nero* | Lucian(?) | Menecrates |
| *Octavia* | Seneca(?) | Octavia |
| *Odyssey* | Homer | Zeus |
| *Orestes* | Euripides | Electra |
| *Parasite* | Lucian | Tychiades |
| *Parmenides* | Plato | Cephalus |
| *Patriot* | Lucian(?) | Triepho |
| *Peace* | Aristophanes | first servant |
| *Persian* | Plautus | Toxilus |
| *Persians* | Aeschylus | chorus |
| *Philebus* | Plato | Socrates |
| *Phoenician Women* | Euripides | Jocasta |
| *Phoenician Women* | Seneca | Oedipus |
| *Phormio* | Terence | Davus |
| *Plutus* | Aristophanes | Cario |
| *Pot of Gold* | Plautus | Euclio |
| *Prometheus Bound* | Aeschylus | power |
| *Protagoras* | Plato | hetairos ("friend") |
| *Pseudolus* | Plautus | Pseudolus |
| *Punica* | Silius Italicus | Hamilcar Barca |
| *Republic* | Plato | Socrates |
| *Rhesus* | Euripides | chorus |
| *Rope* | Plautus | Sceparnio |
| *Runaways* | Lucian | Apollo |
| *Saturnalia* | Lucian | priest |
| *Self-Tormenter* | Terence | Chremes |

| Title | Author | First character to speak |
|---|---|---|
| *Seven against Thebes* | Aeschylus | Eteocles |
| *Sophist* | Plato | Theodorus |
| *Stichus* | Plautus | Panegyris |
| *Suppliant Women* | Aeschylus | chorus |
| *Suppliants* | Euripides | Aethra |
| *Symposium* | Plato | Apollodorus |
| *Theaetetus* | Plato | Euclides |
| *Theages* | Plato | Demodocus |
| *Thesmophoriazusae* | Aristophanes | Mnesilochus |
| *Thyestes* | Seneca | ghost of Tantalus |
| *Timaeus* | Plato | Socrates |
| *Toxaris* | Lucian | Mnesippus |
| *Trinummus* | Plautus | Megaronides |
| *Trojan Women* | Euripides | Poseidon |
| *Truculentus* | Plautus | Diniarchus |
| *Wasps* | Aristophanes | Sosias |
| *Woman of Andros* | Terence | Simo |
| *Woman of Samos* | Menander | Demeas |

*Category Five*

# Miscellaneous Firsts

## *Greek*

*The best time to set sail*

The best time to sail: when a man sees the first shoots at the top of a fig tree in the spring. (Hesiod *Works and Days* 679)

*Death to the first Athenian*

Diogenes Laertius (3.19) relates a story that a certain fourth century B.C. Aeginetan by the name of Charmandrus had passed a law stating that the first Athenian to visit Aegina should be executed. It so happened that the first Athenian to do so (after the enactment of the law) was Plato. He was tried, and acquitted, reputedly on the ground that he was a philosopher.

*The first and only instance of lightning striking twice*

According to Callimachus (as reported by Pliny the Elder 7.152), lightning simultaneously struck statues of the fifth century B.C. boxer Euthymus: one statue was located in Euthymus' hometown, Locri in Italy; the other, in Olympia. This celestial marvel was unprecedented and never duplicated.

*The first blessing for a sailor*

According to Pindar (*Pythian* 1), the first propitious sign for a seaman about to sail is a favorable wind, as if such a phenomenon boded well for the return trip. The poet uses this image in connection with the chariot race champion Hiero, founder of (and first Pythian winner from) the town of Aetna. The hope is that many more champion athletes will emerge from Aetna.

*The first brigand encountered by Theseus*

When Theseus left his hometown of Troezen to journey to Athens, he took a circuitous route that led him through bandit-infested territories. He encountered many violent thugs along the way; the first of these was Periphetes, the "club-bearer." Theseus subdued and killed him, and expropriated his club, as a symbol of his victory over Periphetes.

Although many of the characters whom Theseus met were hostile, not all were; the first people to show him kindness were those of the race of the Phytalidae. They organized a purification ceremony and a banquet for Theseus. (Plutarch *Life of Theseus* 8, 12)

### The first capture of Troy

Although the Homeric version of the Trojan War enjoys the greatest fame, several other successful attacks were made upon Troy prior to the celebrated one. The first of these was led by Telamon, son of Aeacus. (Pindar *Olympian* 8, and note Sandys [LCL] 89)

### The first crown

Diodorus Siculus (4.4) suggests that the custom of royalty adorned with crowns arose from the god Dionysus, who wore a headband as a prophylactic against headaches brought on by excessive drinking.

### The first cultivated roses

The cultivation of roses began as early as the seventh century B.C.; the first reference to cultivated roses dates to 648 B.C. (OCD s.v. gardens)

### The first Cynic

Ausonius (*Epigram* 46) asserts that Antisthenes of Athens was the first Cynic, and founder of the sect. Diogenes Laertius (6.13) adds that Antisthenes was the first noted philosopher to be satisfied with but one cloak and a pouch.

### The first Dorian community

The first Dorian community was reputedly founded by Dorus, the youngest son of Hellen, near Mount Parnassus. (Graves [Vol. I] 158)

### The first Egyptian to use a divine Greek title

The first Egyptian king to use a Greek title — *Theos*, "god" — was Ptolemy XII ("Auletes," first century B.C.) (OCD s.v. Ptolemy XII)

### The first endeavor for a young man

According to Xenophon (*On Hunting* 2.1), the first activity in which a young man should attain proficiency was hunting.

### The first man to enter seven chariots at the Olympic games

Sponsoring a chariot at the Olympic games was an expensive proposition, undertaken only by wealthier Greek citizens. Alcibiades, however, shattered all precedents in this regard, when he entered seven chariots in the games of 416 B.C. Plutarch (*Life of Alcibiades* 11, quoting Thucydides) relates that Alcibiades' chariots took first, second and fourth places.

### The first meat diets for Olympic athletes

In the earliest days of the Olympics, athletes generally adhered to vegetarian diets. The sixth century B.C. boxer Pythagoras of Samos was the first to incorporate meat into his dietary regimen. Pythagoras was also the first man to box *entechnos*, "scientifically," probably meaning that he introduced various combinations of moves, feints and similar strategies. (Diogenes Laertius 8.47; Pliny the Elder 23. 121)

### The first naked Olympic athlete

In the earliest days of the Olympic games, the athletes were clothed. The tradition of competing in the nude is thought to have begun with Orsippus, the winner of the foot race in the Olympics of 720 B.C. (OCD s.v. Orsippus)

### The first name of the Black Sea

The Black Sea was originally called the Axeinus, "unfriendly," because of the hostility of the peoples living on its shores. But the civilizing influence of foreign visitors gradually softened the attitudes of the natives, and the sea's name was changed to Euxinus (or Euxine), "friendly." (DCM s.v. Axine)

### The first of the Seven Sages

A foolish person once asked the Delphic oracle for the identity of the first among the Seven Sages. The oracular response: attach a piece of paper bearing all the names to a ball, so that none could ever appear first (or last) on the list. (Ausonius *Masque of the Seven Sages* [*Solon*] 4)

### The first Olympic winners

According to Pindar (*Olympian* 10), the first Olympic winners were as follows:

| Event | First winner |
| --- | --- |
| stade race | Oeonus of Midea |
| wrestling | Echemus of Tegea |
| boxing | Doryclus of Tiryns |
| four-horse chariot racing | Samos of Mantinea |
| javelin | Phrastor [home not stated] |
| discus | Niceus [home not stated] |

Pindar here refers to the mythological founding of the games by Hercules, and the legendary winners. The first "historically" documented victor was

Coroebus of Elis in the stade race, the only event of the first Olympics in 776 B.C.

### The first palm awarded to victorious athletes
According to Plutarch (*Life of Theseus* 21), Theseus originated the custom of awarding a palm to victorious athletes, at Delos, where he founded athletic contests.

### The first people
Diodorus Siculus (1.8) devotes several paragraphs to a description of the first inhabitants of the world. He characterized them as primitive and ignorant, living a perilous existence, without knowledge of the manner of acquiring the basics of life, such as shelter, warmth, clothing and food. In 1.9, he notes that unspecified *barbaroi* (foreigners) claimed to have been the first to become civilized, the first "to discover the things which are of use in life." (tr. Oldfather [LCL] 33)

Diodorus notes further (1.10) that the Egyptians claimed that the human race originated in Egypt, primarily because of the favorable soil and climate there.

### The first people to colonize the Spanish coast
The first people to found colonies on the Spanish coast were the Phoenicians. Their first colony may have been Tartessus; they also founded Gades. (Harper's s.v. Hispania)

### The first philosopher condemned to death
Socrates was the first philosopher tried before a jury and condemned to death. (Diogenes Laertius 2.20)

### The first "prize" for an athlete
Speaking somewhat metaphorically, Pindar (*Pythian* 1), suggests that the first prize for an athlete is good luck, and the second, a favorable reputation. An athlete who manages to secure both is in the best position of all.

### The first recipient of the tripod
When some fishermen serendipitously retrieved a golden tripod from the Mediterranean, a great ownership dispute arose. Apollo's Delphic oracle decreed that it ought to be given to "the wisest of men." The celebrated Seven Sages were thriving at the time, and it was decided to present the tripod first of all to one of the seven, Thales of Miletus. (Then follows the famous story of Thales, and the other six, all declining the tripod, which ultimately found a home at Delphi.) (Plutarch *Life of Solon* 4)

*The first requirement for a hunting dog*
Xenophon (*On Hunting* 4.1) believed that imposing size was the prime requirement for a good hunting dog.

*The first requirements for a farmer*
Hesiod (*Works and Days* 405–406) suggests that a farmer must begin with two assets: an ox for plowing, and a woman, the latter not for marriage, but to help with plowing and with keeping the farmer's household organized.

*The first to celebrate the Eleusinian Mysteries*
Some versions of Greek mythology credit Erechtheus, the sixth king of Athens, with the founding of the Eleusinian Mysteries. (DCM s.v. Erechtheus)

*The first to combine country and city living*
The philosopher Epicurus (circa 340–270 B.C.) was the first urban homeowner to incorporate extensive gardens into his property. His home and "countrified" grounds in Athens became the site of his philosophical school. (Pliny the Elder 19.51; OCD s.v. Epicurus)

*The first to discover Theseus' identity*
When Theseus arrived in Athens to claim his birthright, he was unknown both to rulers and to citizens. The first to recognize him was the sorceress Medea, who was living at the time with King Aegeus, Theseus' true father. (Plutarch *Life of Theseus* 12)

*The first to receive the title sophos ("sage"; "wise man")*
The first of the Seven Sages to be referred to as *sophos* was Thales of Miletus. The date: 582 B.C. (Diogenes Laertius 1.22)

*The first to separate medicine from philosophy*
In its earliest history, medicine was viewed as a branch of philosophy. The first to separate the two into distinct disciplines was the celebrated physician Hippocrates. (Celsus *On Medicine: Introduction* 8)

*The first to taste the special brew*
Each autumn, a festival called the Oschophoria was celebrated in Athens. Among other events, it featured a foot race involving prominent Athenian young men. The winner of this race received the privilege of being allowed the first taste of a specially prepared liquid concoction called the *pentaploa*, [one containing] "five ingredients." (OCD s.v. Oschophoria)

*The first victim of the bronze bull*

Phalaris, sixth century B.C. tyrant of Agrigentum in Sicily, commissioned the sculptor Perillus to fashion a bronze bull. Perillus agreed, "guaranteeing that if a man were shut up inside it, and a fire lit underneath, the man would do the bellowing." In an apparent effort to test the sculptor's boast, Phalaris made him the first victim. (Pliny the Elder 34.89; tr. Rackham Vol. IX [LCL] 193; Harper's s.v. Phalaris)

*Four firsts and onlys*

According to Pliny the Elder (7.133), the Spartan Lampido was history's first and only woman to have been the daughter, wife and mother of a king, while Berenice enjoyed the status of first and only daughter, sister and mother of champion Olympic athletes. Among the Romans, only the Curio family had three celebrated orators, while the Fabian family was the first and only to boast of three consecutive generations of *principes senatus*, heads of the Senate.

Of these four examples, Pliny names the individuals of only the last: Marcus Fabius Ambustus, his son Quintus Fabius Rullianus, and (Marcus') grandson, Quintus Fabius Gurges (fl. fourth century B.C.). (OCD s.v. Fabius Ambustus, Marcus)

*A hierarchy of greater (divine) and lesser (human) goods*

In creating a rank ordering of desirable divine goods, wisdom comes first; in human goods, health takes the first place. (Plato *Laws* I 631B, C)

*The holiness of the first day of the month*

According to Hesiod (*Works and Days* 770–771), the first, fourth and seventh days of each month are to be considered holy.

*"Last of the Crotoniates, but first of the Greeks"*

This proverb alluded to the running prowess of athletes from Croton, a Greek colony in southern Italy. The saying gained prominence after one of the first Olympics, in which the first seven finishers in the stade (200-yard) race were all natives of Croton; hence, the last Crotoniate was faster than the fastest of the rest of the Greeks. (Strabo 6.1)

*A pilgrimage for the first haircut*

According to Plutarch (*Life of Theseus* 5), it was customary in Theseus' time for youths to make a sacrificial journey to Delphi, where their hair was cut for the first time. Plutarch adds that the Abantes were the first people to observe this custom.

*Plato's first name*

According to Diogenes Laertius (3.4), Plato was originally named Aristocles, his grandfather's name. Diogenes relates several stories about the source of the name Plato ("broad," "wide"); one of these stories refers to his physique (broad-shouldered), another to the breadth of his writing style.

Aristocles was used in one of the epitaphs on his tomb. (Diogenes Laertius 3.43)

### Plato's first visit to Sicily

According to Diogenes Laertius (3.18), Plato made three voyages to Sicily. His purposes in traveling there the first time were two-fold: to see the island, and to visit Mount Aetna.

### The primacy of Egypt

Diodorus Siculus (1.9) states that he began his treatise on world history with Egypt, because Egypt was thought to have been home to the first gods, and because the first astronomical observations were reportedly undertaken there.

### The primacy of Sicily

In Book V of his history of the world, Diodorus Siculus discusses islands. First in the discussion was Sicily, which was first among all Mediterranean islands in terms of the respect accorded to it.

The original name of Sicily: Trinacria ("three capes," a reference to the three promontories formed by the island's triangular shape.) The first people to dwell there were called the Sicani. Thucydides (6.2) reports that the Cyclopes and Laestrygonians were the island's first residents, although he also notes that the Sicanians claimed that distinction.

The first Greeks to settle in Sicily hailed from Euboea. (Thucydides 6.3)

### A snake's first weapon

Diodorus Siculus (3.36–37) describes amazing African snakes, some reputedly large enough that, when coiled, resembled a small hill. He claims that the largest of these reptiles would attack and eat oxen, bulls, and even elephants. The snakes' first strategy: to entangle the legs of their intended prey, and then raise their heads to eye level with the victim's head; next, to emit extremely bright flashes of light from their eyes, thus blinding the prey and facilitating the kill.

### Socrates' first wife

Most sources indicate that Socrates' first wife was Xanthippe, and his second, Myrto. Others claim the opposite, while still others assert that he was married to both women simultaneously.

His first child was apparently a son named Lamprocles, by Xanthippe. (Diogenes Laertius 2.26)

### Theseus' first burial site

Theseus died, or was murdered, in Scyros, where he was buried. The fifth century (B.C.) general Cimon claimed to have located Theseus' grave and transported the remains to Athens for reburial. (Plutarch *Life of Theseus* 36)

## Roman

### Augustus' first residence in Rome

Augustus first lived in a modest house near the forum; later, he resided on the Palatine Hill, in the former home of the noted first century B.C. orator Quintus Hortensius. (Suetonius *Life of Augustus* 72)

### Augustus' first task

The first post-tyrannicide task which fell to the young Augustus was the avenging of Julius Caesar's murder. (Ovid *Fasti* 3.709–710)

### The dole's pecking order

Under the empire, it became common practice for wealthy patrons to supply their retainers with gifts in little baskets, *sportulae*. Juvenal (1.101 ff.) suggests that there existed a sort of hierarchal structure for receiving the contents of the *sportula*: a praetor first, then a tribune, last a freedman, even if the freedman were first in line when a patron offered the largesse in the morning.

### Elephantine firsts

The first time elephants appeared in Italy occurred in 280 B.C., during the wars with King Pyrrhus. The natives called them *boves Lucae*, "Lucan cattle," because they were first observed in Lucania. Elephants made their first appearance in Rome a few years later, in 275, during a triumphal procession.

The first elephants used in mock battles performed in the Circus Maximus, in 99 B.C. The first time an elephant was matched with a bull in the public arena took place in 79. (Pliny the Elder 8.16, 19)

### Farming firsts

In Book IV of his *Georgics*, Vergil refers to an elderly Corycian (not named) who recorded these firsts:

1. He was the first to pick roses in the spring, the first to harvest apples in the fall.
2. He was the first successful beekeeper, and the first to collect honey from the hives.

*The first altar dedicated to Augustus at Lugdunum*

On August 1, 13 B.C., the first altar at Lugdunum honoring Augustus was dedicated. Three years later, to the day, the future emperor Claudius was born there. (Suetonius *Life of Claudius* 2)

*The first—and only—man to speak 22 languages*

King Mithridates VI was reputed to be the first and only man fluent in 22 languages; Pliny the Elder (25.6) records that over the course of Mithridates' 56-year reign, he never required the services of an interpreter when conversing with any of his subject peoples.

*The first appearance of Galeria Copiola*

The actress Galeria Copiola made her acting debut in 82 B.C. Ninety-one years later, at the age of 104, she appeared at games dedicated to the recovery of health of the emperor Augustus. (Pliny the Elder 7.158)

*The first artificial gold and silver foliage*

Marcus Licinius Crassus was the first to fabricate leaves of gold and silver, which he incorporated into small crowns awarded to victorious performances at the games which he sponsored. (Pliny the Elder 21.6)

*The first aviary*

The first enclosure for birds was built by a Brundisian named Marcus Laenius Strabo. He placed this giant birdcage in the peristyle of his home, and fed its occupants through a net which enveloped the entire structure. (Varro *On Agriculture* 3.5)

*The first benefactor in the alimenta system*

The *alimenta* was a kind of charitable system, funded by wealthy individuals (primarily through interest on mortgage payments) to assist children in need. The first known benefactor was a certain Titus Julius Helvia, who lived in the middle of the first century A.D. (OCD s.v. *alimenta*)

*The first brother to see birds*

When Romulus and Remus decided to utilize augury to determine which of the two would found Rome, Remus was the first to observe birds: six vultures, according to Livy (1.7).

*The first bullfight*

In 45 B.C., Julius Caesar introduced into public shows a new event in which a mounted rider guided his galloping horse close by a running bull. The rider then attempted to grab the bull's horns and twist its neck backward, thus killing it. (Pliny the Elder 8.182)

### The first celebration of a lectisternium

The winter of 400-399 B.C. was unusually cold and snowy in Rome; as a consequence, it was decided that special propitiation needed to be made to the gods. Hence, the initiation of the *lectisternium* ("spread the couch"), an eight-day ceremony honoring Apollo, Latona, Diana, Hercules, Mercury, and Neptune, with three couches adorned with food and offerings for them. (Livy 5.13)

### The first celebration of the Floralia

Festivals honoring crops and vegetation were obviously important in agrarian societies. The Romans celebrated several of these, including the Robigalia, first observed on April 25, circa 704 B.C., and the Floralia, initially celebrated on April 23 of 238. (Pliny the Elder 18.285–286)

### The first celebration of the Ludi Sullanae Victoriae

The games in honor of the Sullan victory were instituted and celebrated by Sulla for the first time in 82 B.C., after his siege and conquest of the younger Marius at Praeneste. (Velleius Paterculus 2.27)

### The first city in Italy

Appian (*Civil War* 2.20) records the tradition that Lanuvium was the first city founded in Italy, by Diomedes who immigrated there after the Trojan War. Lanuvium (located about 20 miles from Rome) was the birthplace of two prominent first century B.C. figures: the politician Titus Annius Milo, and the actor Quintus Roscius Gallus. The second century A.D. emperor Antoninus Pius was also born there.

### The first civilian use of the title princeps juventutis

The *princeps juventutis* ("chief of the youth") was originally a military title conferred upon the commander of equestrians who were under the age of 45. It was first used in a civilian context by Augustus, who gave the designation to his grandsons, Gaius and Lucius Caesar, the implication being that they were to be his imperial successors. (Rolfe Suetonius Vol. I [LCL] 424)

### The first cloak-clad emperor to preside at gladiatorial games

According to Suetonius (*Life of Claudius* 2), the emperor Claudius wore a cloak while presiding over gladiatorial games — a first. Suetonius asserts that Claudius' ill health inspired this precedent.

### The first craftsmen's wares

Juvenal (15.166–168) laments that the earliest craftsmen produced metal farm implements, and did not even know how to make the weapons of war, such as swords. But in Juvenal's day, he says, people seem to want swords capable of not merely slaying an enemy, but dismembering him.

### The first day of the Roman month

The first day of every Roman month was called the *Kalendae* (Kalends; cf. English "calendar." The fifteenth day in the months of March, May, October and July was called the *Ides*; hence, the Ides of March — March 15. In the other eight months, the Ides fell on the thirteenth day.)

### The first days of each season

According to Varro (*On Agriculture* 1.28), the first days of each season occur as follows:

| Season | Sign in which the first day occurs |
| --- | --- |
| Spring | Aquarius |
| Summer | Taurus |
| Autumn | Leo |
| Winter | Scorpio |

### The first day's torture

One of the emperor Nero's torture victims — a woman named Epicharis, implicated in plotting against him — suffered the following on her first day of captivity: she was placed on a rack, where she was whipped and burned, and suffered dislocated limbs. When she refused to capitulate to this inhumane treatment, a second day of torture was planned. However, she managed to commit suicide before any more pain could be inflicted upon her. (Tacitus *Annals* 15.57)

### The first dinner item

Banqueters at formal dinners were often served eggs as their first consumables. (Varro *On Agriculture* 1.2)

### The first Dives ("Rich")

The first Roman known by the cognomen Dives was the first century B.C. multimillionaire Marcus Licinius Crassus. He was also the first Roman whose principal claim to fame was his great wealth. (Pliny the Elder 33.134)

### The first division of agriculture

According to Varro (*On Agriculture* 1.5), agricultural knowledge could be organized into four main areas, the first of which was *cognitio fundi*, "an understanding of the farm"; this included knowledge of soil types and farm buildings. (The other three divisions: farm equipment; plowing; seasons for plowing.)

### The first domesticated animals

Varro (*On Agriculture* 2.2) claims that sheep were the first animals to be captured and domesticated.

### The first elaborate dining room furniture

In 187 B.C., Gnaeus Manlius became the first Roman to decorate a dining room with luxurious furniture, such as "dinner couches and panelled sideboards and one-leg tables decorated with bronze." (Pliny the Elder 34.14; tr. Rackham Vol. IX [LCL] 137)

### The first emperor to devalue Roman coinage

The value of the basic Roman coin, the *denarius*, had remained constant since the third century B.C.; the emperor Nero, however, reduced both the weight and the silver content of the *denarius*, thus becoming the first emperor to do so. Modern scholars offer several reasons for this, but the most compelling of these may be that a decline in the production of precious metals necessitated Nero's action. (Boren 213)

### The first farm-bred livestock

The first animals raised on farms were actually birds: chickens. Roman soothsayers used chickens during the course of their various auguries, and so a ready supply of the birds was deemed necessary. (Varro *On Agriculture* 3.3)

### The first food of Latium

Pliny the Elder (18.83) asserts that the first food consumed by the earliest inhabitants of Latium was starch.

### A first for the new emperor Claudius

When the emperor Claudius appeared in the forum bearing for the first time the trappings of his imperial office, an eagle that was flying past landed on his right shoulder — a propitious sign for the new reign. (Suetonius *Life of Claudius* 7)

### The first force for decency

According to Ovid, Venus first caused men to dress decently and to observe appropriate hygienic standards (thus better to attract female companionship!). (*Fasti* 4.107–108. In 113, Ovid asserts that Venus was the inventor of *mille artes*, "a thousand arts.")

### The first formal gardens

Lucius Licinius Lucullus was the first Roman to own and cultivate extensive pleasure gardens (the *horti Lucullani*). (OCD s.v. gardens)

*The first free banquet at a gladiatorial show*
According to Suetonius (*Life of Claudius* 21), the emperor Claudius was the first Roman government official to provide the spectators a dinner along with the gladiatorial show.

*The first game farm*
The first Roman to confine wild pigs and other animals in game preserves was Fulvius Lippinus (date uncertain). (Pliny the Elder 8.211)

*The first hour of the Roman day*
The first hour of a Roman day was 6:00 to 7:00 A.M., although the 12 hours of the day were shorter in winter, longer in summer. (Balsdon 18)

*The first indication of Bacchic rites in Italy*
A fifth century (B.C.) inscription discovered at Cumae is the earliest evidence of Bacchic activity in Italy. The text deals with burial sites for initiates and non-initiates. (OCD s.v. Bacchanalia)

*The first item in a petitionary prayer*
Juvenal (10.23) remarks that the first and most frequent prayer heard in the gods' temples is for wealth and more wealth.

*The first king of Troy*
According to most mythological versions, Troy's first king was Teucer; hence, the Trojans were sometimes called the Teucrians. (DCM s.v. Teucer)

*The first land allotments*
Romulus was said to have first allotted two iugera of land per citizen; and this was the maximum amount which could be passed on to heirs. (Varro *On Agriculture* 1.10)

*The first letter as an omen*
It is said that Augustus' death was foretold by several signs. One of these: lightning struck and destroyed the first letter of his title (Caesar), which had been inscribed on one of his statues. The soothsayers interpreted this to mean that he had but 100 days left to live, since "C," of course, is the Roman numeral for 100. (Suetonius *Life of Augustus* 97)

*The first Ludi Apollinares*
The first games in honor of Apollo were celebrated in 212 B.C., under the sponsorship of the praetor Publius Cornelius Sulla. (Livy 27.23; MRR Vol. I 268)

*The first Maximus*

The first Roman to bear the cognomen Maximus (Greatest) was Marcus Valerius. He earned the name through his efforts in bringing a peaceable conclusion to the first secession of the plebeians, in 494 B.C. (Cicero *Brutus* 54)

*The first meal of the day*

The Roman equivalent of breakfast —*jentaculum*— was generally a modest meal, limited perhaps to staples like bread and cheese. (Balsdon 20)

*The first moon and the last moon*

The Romans observed the waxing and the waning of the moon, and called the point precisely between the waning of the full moon and the onset of the new as the *intermenstruum*, "between months," or the *extrema et prima*, "last and first." (Varro *On Agriculture* 1.37)

*The first multiple exhibitions of lions*

Quintus Mucius Scaevola was the first to introduce into shows fights involving more than one lion. Scaevola, the preeminent lawyer of his time (early first century B.C.) was the first legal scholar "to give serious consideration to classification ... e.g. five types of guardianship." (OCD s.v. Mucius Scaevola [2], Quintus)

In 93 B.C., Lucius Cornelius Sulla became the first to display lions in great numbers: 100, in one of the shows which he sponsored. (Pliny the Elder 8.53)

*The first name of Baiae*

The Roman resort town of Baiae was originally named Aquae Cumanae, a reference to the hot springs which proliferated in the area. (Harper's s.v. Baiae)

*The first name of Beneventum*

The Campanian town of Beneventum was originally called Maleventum; tradition has it, however, that the name was changed to Beneventum because of the sinister association with the word *male* (evil). The changeover occurred in 271 B.C. (Livy 9.27 ; Harper's s.v. Beneventum)

*The first notable Octavius*

The first member of Augustus' gens to be elected to office was a certain Gaius (or Gnaeus) Octavius Rufus, chosen as quaestor in 230 B.C. (Suetonius *Life of Augustus* 2; MRR Vol. I 227)

*The first noted wine vintage*

The first known noted wines dated from the consulship of Opimius, in 121 B.C. Wine was expensive; therefore, only one vintage was generally served at most dinners. However, at a banquet in 46 B.C., Julius Caesar became the first Roman to offer his guests four: Falernian, Chian, Lesbian and Mamertine. (Balsdon 43–44)

*The first of the Ptolemaic rulers to learn Egyptian*

The first of the Ptolemaic (i.e., Macedonian) rulers of Egypt to learn the Egyptian language was Cleopatra VII, a rather remarkable achievement given that her family had ruled Egypt for almost 300 years prior to her time. She was also fluent in several other languages. (OCD s.v. Cleopatra VII)

*The first perfumes*

Pliny the Elder (13.2) admitted that he did not know who invented perfume, but he speculated that the Persians might have done so; the first indication (of which he was aware) in support of this suspicion: Alexander the Great's capture of a cache of perfumes from the property of the Persian King Darius III (reigned fourth century B.C.).

*The first politician to provide free grain*

During his tribunate (58 B.C.), Publius Clodius provided free grain to the populace, a precedent-setting action. (Boren 127, 141)

*The first Porcius of note*

The first noted member of the Porcian family was Cato the Elder (circa 234–149 B.C.). Pliny the Elder (7.100) suggests that Cato was the first to excel in the three most significant areas of achievement open to an ancient Roman: as an orator, a soldier, and a senator.

*The first portraits in libraries*

The first Roman to display bronze likenesses of noted personages in libraries was Gaius Asinius Pollio, in the 30s B.C. (Pliny the Elder 35.10)

*The first priestess of Fortuna Muliebris*

After a delegation of Roman women had induced Gaius Marcius Coriolanus to end his hostile designs on Rome, the grateful Senate decreed the construction of an altar and a temple dedicated to Fortuna Muliebris. The first priestess of the new temple was Valeria, one of the leaders of the delegation. (Dionysius of Halicarnassus 8.55)

### The first recipient of the title Augusta

The honorary title Augusta was first conferred upon Livia, the emperor Augustus' widow, by the terms of his will. (OCD s.v. Augustus, Augusta as titles)

### The first reference to a seven-day week

An inscription (CIL 1.220, dated between 19 B.C. and A.D. 14) preserving the remains of a Sabine calendar is the earliest known public record of a seven-day week. The calendar (as reproduced by Balsdon 62):

| | | | |
|---|---|---|---|
| E | A | F | Where the first column represents the seven |
| F | B | N | days, the second column the *nundinum* |
| G | C | C | (eight-day cycle in which the eighth day was |
| A | D | C | a market day); the third column represents |
| B | E | C | days on which business could or could not be |
| C | F | C | transacted. *F(aestus)* and *C(omitalis)* were |
| D | G | C | legal business days; *N(efastus)* was not. |
| E | H | C | |
| F | A | C | |

### The first requirement of beekeeping

A farmer wishing to raise and keep bees should first seek a sheltered place for the hives, one protected from winds and curious or clumsy animals. (Vergil *Georgics* 4)

### The first requirements for various farm animals

The main consideration for a farmer pondering the acquisition of four-footed animals: to purchase an ox suitable for plowing (Varro *On Agriculture* 1.20). When purchasing geese, the most important characteristics which one must consider are their size (plump) and color (white; Varro 3.9).

The first consideration for a duck farm: a marshy location (Varro 3.11). And a person intent on starting any kind of farm must take into account many requirements; the first and most important of these: deciding which kinds of animals or fowl would be the most enjoyable and profitable to raise. (Varro 3.3)

### The first riser on the farm

Cato the Elder (*On Agriculture* 5) maintains that the overseer (*vilicus*) of a farm ought to be the first man to arise in the morning, and the last to go to bed at night.

### The first Roman mint

Although the Romans used coins and other means of exchange prior to the third century B.C., a formal mint was first established in about 289. The first metal used in Roman currency was bronze. Silver was employed for the first time in 269; gold coins made their first appearance during the Second Punic War (218–202). (OCD s.v. coinage, Roman)

### The first Roman to cultivate oysters

Lucius Sergius Orata was the first Roman to cultivate oysters in specially constructed ponds, circa 90 B.C. He reportedly profitted greatly from this innovation. He also became something of an oyster connoisseur, and he was the first Roman to rate the quality of oysters. In his opinion, the best ones were to be found in the Lucrine Lake.

Orata was also the first Roman to devise showers for home use. He apparently derived a part of his income by selling and installing showers in the bathrooms of upscale county villas. (Pliny the Elder 9.168; 170)

### The first Roman to display justitia and temperantia

Gnaeus Cornelius Scipio, a Punic War general who commanded Roman armies in Spain between 218 and 211, was greatly mourned upon his battlefield death. He earned the respect and affection of his men partially because of his just and temperate qualities ( *justitia* and *temperantia*); Livy (25.36) asserts that Scipio was the first Roman official to display these virtues.

### The first Roman to divorce his wife

The first Roman of note to divorce his wife was a certain Spurius Carvilius Ruga; his grounds: he claimed that the married in order to have children, and that his divorce action was justified because his wife was barren. The year is uncertain, with authorities such as Valerius Maximus (604 B.C.) and Dionysius of Halicarnassus (231 B.C.) suggesting widely varying dates.

### The first Roman to shave regularly

According to Pliny the Elder, the first Roman to allow his chin to go under the razor on a daily basis was Scipio Africanus.

### The first row of seats for senators

When a senator appeared to view entertainments in a crowded amphitheater in Puteoli, and none of the spectators offered him a seat, Augustus enacted a measure reserving the front row of seats in theaters and amphitheaters for senators. (Suetonius *Life of Augustus* 44)

### The first shave

For Roman males, the first shaving of their beards represented their initiation into manhood; this was considered a milestone, and was often marked by a family celebration. (Harper's s.v. *barba*)

*The first silver accessories in the arena*

Julius Caesar was the first to decorate an arena with silver accessories (for funeral games in honor of his father, in 65 B.C.). This was also the first time in which wild beast fighters used armor and weaponry fashioned exclusively of silver. (Pliny the Elder 33.53)

*The first silver-plated bedsteads*

An early first century B.C. Roman knight named Carvilius Pollio was the first to own silver-plated bedsteads; he also had the gold-plated variety. (Pliny the Elder 33.141)

*The first step in breaking oxen to the plow*

Unbroken oxen should first drag plows through light, sandy soil on level ground, until they become accustomed to the work. Similarly, cattle should first be hitched to empty wagons before they are expected to pull full loads. (Varro *On Agriculture* 1.20)

*The first to attempt an accounting of the Varian disaster*

In A.D. 9, the Roman general Publius Quinctilius Varus suffered a crushing military defeat, with many Roman soldiers unaccounted for. The first man to attempt to gather the remains — some years later — and give them a proper burial was Germanicus. (Suetonius *Life of Caligula* 3)

*The first to dedicate cinnamon crowns*

The first authority figure to dedicate gilded cinnamon crowns was Vespasian, on the occasion of consecrating the crowns at the Temples of the Capitol and Peace. (Pliny the Elder 12.94)

*The first to dedicate portrait shields*

According to Pliny the Elder (35.12), Appius Claudius (consul in 495 B.C.) was the first Roman to publicly display shields with portraits, in this instance, in the Temple of Bellona. The portraits were those of his own ancestors, whom he wished to be immortalized in this way.

*The first to discover antidotes to poison*

King Mithridates VI (first century B.C.) was the first to concoct antidotes to poisons. One of his original remedies involved blending the blood of Pontic ducks into the mixture, because they habitually ingested the poisons for which the antidote was prepared, and so acquired a natural immunity. (Pliny the Elder 25.4–6)

*The first to establish a fixed date for the Games of Apollo*

The games of Apollo, instituted in 212 B.C., were originally held annually, but not on any specific calendar date. In 208 however, a pestilence struck; it was decided that the games ought to be celebrated on a fixed date. The first official to vow and supervise the games under this condition was the city praetor, Publius Licinius Varus. (Livy 27.23)

*The first to kiss his mother*

Lucius Junius Brutus accompanied two sons of Tarquinius Superbus to the oracle at Delphi. Among other things, the two sons wished to know which of them would become the next ruler in Rome. The reply: "He will have supreme power in Rome who first, young men, lays a kiss upon his mother." The brothers decided to employ a lottery system to determine which of them would kiss their mother first, upon their return to Rome. Brutus, however, interpreted the oracular response to refer to Mother Earth. He immediately pretended to trip and fell to the ground, in the process brushing the dirt with his lips. He thus became the "first to lay a kiss upon his mother," and he did indeed eventually become Rome's first consul. (Livy 1.56)

*The first to offer sacrifices to the gods*

In the Ovidian account (*Fasti* 1.337–352), Ceres is identified as the first to carry out an animal sacrifice. She killed a sow as an act of vengeance because the beast had consumed the seeds which she had sown during the spring planting season.

*The first to organize a three-part contest*

The emperor Nero organized the first quinquennial, Greek-style, three-part contest at Rome. The three components: music, gymnastics, and horse-back riding. He named the entire event after himself: the Neronia. (Suetonius *Life of Nero* 12)

*The first to own 1,000 pounds of silver*

The first Roman to count among his possessions 1,000 pounds of silver was Quintus Fabius Maximus Allobrogicus, consul in 121 B.C. (Pliny the Elder 33.141)

*The first to serve Alban grapes and wine-dregs with caviar*

The first (possibly fictional) gourmand Catius bragged that he was "the first to serve [Alban grapes] round the board with apples ... and the first to serve up wine-lees and caviare [sic]" (tr. Fairclough [LCL] 193), as well as salt and pepper on side dishes. (Horace *Satires* 2.4.73–75). In *Satire* 2.8.51, Fundanius similarly boasts that he was the first to show that "one should boil in [wine and fish] sauce green rockets and bitter elecampane." (tr. Fairclough [LCL] 243)

### *The first to serve whole boars at banquets*
The early Romans were suspicious of consuming boar's meat, but by the first century B.C., it had become something of a luxury. The first to serve a whole boar to his guests was Publius Servilius Rullus. By Pliny the Elder's time, it was not uncommon for two, or even three boars to be eaten at a banquet, sometimes as the first course. (Pliny the Elder 8.210)

### *The first to term Trajan optimus princeps*
Pliny the Younger is thought to have been the first Roman to apply to Trajan the title *optimus princeps* ("best [first] citizen"). (Boren 238)

### *The first to use dyed linen*
Pliny the Elder (19.22–23) states that Alexander the Great was the first person of note to use dyed linen for sails and bunting on ships; Alexander's subordinates, in fact, habitually competed with one another to see who could display the most colorful array of sails.

Quintus Lutatius Catulus (first century B.C.) was the first Roman to use linen for large-scale awnings; his contemporary, Publius Cornelius Lentulus Spinther, initiated the use of linen awnings in theaters.

### *The first to wear a purple-bordered robe*
The first king to wear a robe displaying a purple border with a prominent purple stripe was Tullus Hostilius (reigned circa 671–642 B.C.). The first politician to use (the very expensive) Tyrian purple dye for a robe was Publius Cornelius Lentulus Spinther (consul 57 B.C.) (Pliny the Elder 9.136, 137)

### *The first toga-clad actor*
The actor Stephanio (fl. first century A.D.) was the first to appear on stage *togatus*, "dressed in a toga." (Pliny the Elder 7.159)

### *The first Torquatus*
The first holder of the cognomen Torquatus was Tiberius Manlius. He reputedly obtained the title by defeating a Celt in single combat (361 B.C.) and appropriating his collar (*torques*). His third century B.C. descendant, also named Tiberius Manlius Torquatus, was the only Roman official in the 700-year span between Numa and Augustus to close Janus' temple gates (a symbol of peace); the date: 235 B.C. (OCD s.v. Torquatus [1 and 2])

*The first tree pruner*

The first Roman to devise a method of pruning plane trees was Gaius Matius, a contemporary of Augustus. (Pliny the Elder 12.13)

*The first "university"*

About A.D. 135, the emperor Hadrian established Rome's first public institution of what moderns would call higher education: the Athenaeum. The structure resembled a theater, and served as the locale for (salaried) rhetoricians, philosophers, poets, lawyers and others, to give lectures and recitations. (Harper's s.v. Athenaeum)

*The first use of the word "peninsula"*

Livy was the first Roman author to combine the words *paene* (almost) and *insula* (island) into one: *paeninsula*. He used the word in the course of his description of the location of New Carthage, on the Spanish coast (26.42).

*The first Vestal Virgin*

When a young girl became a Vestal Virgin, the pontifex maximus called her *Amata* in the formulaic ritual whereby she formally entered Vesta's service. According to Aulus Gellius (1.12), the appellation *Amata* was used because the first Vestal Virgin was reportedly named Amata.

*The first woman judged to be the most chaste*

In 114 B.C., a unique election was held, to select from among 100 candidates the *pudicissima femina*, "most chaste woman." Sulpicia, winner of the vote, was the first Roman woman so honored. The election was held for the purpose of choosing a woman to dedicate a statue of Venus. (Pliny the Elder 7.120)

*The initial greeting of the day*

Martial indicates (3.95) that a person's first greeter of the day is frequently a cawing crow, not a fellow human. The poet occasionally complains about friends and acquaintances who never offer the first greeting when he meets them on the street, but who wait for Martial to take the salutation initiative (e.g., 5.66)

*A Jugurthine first*

The Numidian king Jugurtha prided himself on his physical prowess. According to Sallust (*Jugurtha* 6), when he went forth on a hunting expedition, he was invariably the first, or one of the first, to shoot a lion or other hunted beast.

*Julius Caesar's first residence in Rome*

Julius Caesar first resided in the Subura, a rough and crime-ridden slum area in the center of the city. After he was elected pontifex maximus, he moved to the Regia, the official residence provided for the holder of that office. (Suetonius *Life of Julius Caesar* 46)

*A litigant's first expectation*

According to Juvenal (7.139–141), when a litigant hires a lawyer, the first consideration is not the lawyer's knowledge or eloquence, but his wealth. The poet sarcastically remarks that even the golden-tongued Cicero (who predated Juvenal's time by a century and a half) would have a difficult time securing legal work in Juvenal's Rome unless he sported an expensive ring on his finger.

In another poem (3.126 ff.), Juvenal suggests that the first question asked about a witness in a court case customarily pertains not to his character, but to his wealth: "A man's word is believed in proportion to the amount of cash he keeps in his strongbox." (tr. Ramsay [LCL] 43)

*The medicinal properties of a child's first lost tooth*

Pliny the Elder (28.41) relates the story that if a woman were to retrieve the first tooth lost by a child, and attach it to a bracelet worn continuously on her arm, that it could protect her from genital discomfort — providing the tooth had never fallen to the ground.

*Mount Vesuvius' first eruption*

The first recorded volcanic eruption of Mount Vesuvius was also the catastrophic one in the summer of A.D. 79, which destroyed the cities of Pompeii and Herculaneum. Three later eruptions occurred, in 202, 472 and 512. Mount Aetna's (Sicily) first documented eruption took place in 475 B.C. (OCD s.vv. Aetna; Vesuvius)

*The name of the first month*

*Mensis Januarius*— the month of January — derives its name from Janus, the Roman god of beginnings. (DCM s.v. Janus)

*No first names for women*

Roman women did not receive *praenomina* (as did males), but rather, they generally assumed the feminized form of the father's *nomen* (e.g., Gaius Julius Caesar's daughter's name was Julia. Plutarch *Life of Marius* 1).

*The occasion of Jupiter's first weaponry*

Jupiter was originally conceived of as an unarmed god. He first took up his celebrated thunderbolts to battle the Titans for control of the universe. (Ovid *Fasti* 3.437–440)

### The primacy of money

According to Horace (*Epistles* 1.1), an unofficial motto of Rome's business community ran: *O cives, cives, quaerenda pecunia primum est; virtus post nummos*: "Citizens, citizens, seek money first; virtue after the Almighty Dollar [or Sestertium?]."

### The provider of Jupiter's first meal

Ovid (*Fasti* 3.659–660) reports that some ancients believed that the nymph Anna Perenna was the first to provide food for Jupiter.

### Scaurus' show-time firsts

Marcus Aemilius Scaurus claimed two firsts while aedile in 58 B.C.:

1. He was the first to exhibit a large number of female leopards, 150 of them.
2. He was the first to display in Rome a hippopotamus and five crocodiles. (Pliny the Elder 8.64, 96)

Also, no Roman before Scaurus possessed a collection of precious stones; he was the first. (Pliny 37.11)

### Seneca's catalogue of firsts

In his essay *On the Shortness of Life* (12), the philosopher Seneca recounts a number of Roman firsts, famous and otherwise:

1. The first general to win a naval battle: Gaius Duillius.
2. The first general to display elephants in a triumphal procession: Curius Dentatus.
3. The first general to develop a strong navy and encourage its use: Claudius Caudex.
4. The first general to subdue Messana (in Sicily): Manius Valerius Corvinus, who was also the first man in his family to use the cognomen Messana, later emended to Messalla.
5. The first to put lions on display in the circus: Lucius Cornelius Sulla. His younger contemporary Pompey initiated the display — and slaughter — of elephants in the circus.

### Two dinner party firsts

1. The orator Quintus Hortensius was the first host to offer his guests peacock at an augural dinner. (Balsdon 37; Macrobius 3.13)
2. The father of Publius Servilius Rullus (tribune 63 B.C.) was the

first to serve a whole boar at a dinner party. (Balsdon 37; Pliny the Elder 8.210)

### The varied meanings of primus

The Latin word *primus*, whose basic meaning, of course, is "first," also had numerous idiomatic usages, including:

| Latin phrase | Literal meaning | Free translation |
|---|---|---|
| 1. *primi dentes* | first teeth | front teeth |
| 2. *prima fercula* | first dishes | first course at a dinner |
| 3. *prima fronte* | by the first front | outwardly; superficially |
| 4. *primus gradus* | first rank | front row in a theater, etc. |
| 5. *primus grex* | first flock | first rank, especially of slaves |
| 6. *prima luce* | at first light | dawn; sunrise |
| 7. *primo mane* | in the first morning | early in the morning |
| 8. *primus ordo* | first rank | first rank of soldiers |
| 9. *primae partes* | first parts | the leading role in a stage play |
| 10. *primi pedes* | first feet | front feet of animals |
| 11. *primus pilus* | first cohort (of a legion) | the word eventually came to refer to the top-ranking centurion of a legion: *primipilus* |
| 12. *prima subsellia* | first seats | front seats in a theater, etc. |
| 13. *primum tempus* | first (in) time | the earliest |

Other expressions include: *cum primis*, "with the first," or first of all; most importantly; and *quam primum* "as first [as possible]," or as soon as possible.

*Primus* can also mean "young," or "in the early stages": *primae flammae*, the "first flames" of a newly lit fire; *primae herbae*, the "first [sprouting of] grasses, or crops."

Another meaning for the word: "nearest": *prima ora Graecia*, "nearest shores of Greece"; *primi fines*, "nearest boundary; frontier."

When *primus* was applied to a citizen, or citizens, as an adjective, it meant first in the sense of most eminent, leading.

Similarly, *primus* sometimes means "first-rate," or "best": *primus ager*, "best agricultural land"; *primum medicamentum*, "best remedy."

### When second or third is as respectable as first

Cicero claims that any person who wholeheartedly pushes for excellence should not be disappointed or dismayed if he fails to be acclaimed in the first rank, "for it is no disgrace for one who is striving for the first place to stop at second or third." As an example, he notes that Homer, Archilochus, Sophocles and Pindar are all first-rate poets, but that fact alone does not preclude others from becoming skilled and respected second or third tier poets. (Cicero *On the Orator* 4; tr. Hubbell [LCL] 309)

*Category Six*

# Innovations and Inventions of Noted Individuals

## Greek

*The innovations of Charondas the Thurian* (according to Diodorus Siculus)

Although many of Charondas' legal innovations are now regarded as apocryphal (OCD s.v. Charondas, for example), Diodorus Siculus straightforwardly describes this sixth century B.C. lawgiver's central role in devising the following:

1. Men who remarried and gave their new spouses authority over their children should be permitted no role in politics. His reasoning: a man who so mismanaged his personal affairs could not be trusted with the management of public affairs.
2. Those convicted of bearing false witness were to be punished by the wearing of a tamarisk crown, as a sort of public disgrace.
3. Charondas wrote a unique law prohibiting upright citizens from "friendship and intimacy with unprincipled persons" (tr. Oldfather Vol. II [LCL] 399); the lawgiver feared that evil persons could corrupt the good ones, and that solid citizens could easily be turned to a life of crime and perversion through associating with the dregs of society.
4. Another unprecedented law promulgated by Charondas: he decreed that all young citizens must learn to read and write, and that teachers were to be hired and funded by the state. Charondas placed a very high premium on literacy, since without it,

citizens could not vote, deal in correspondence, or understand laws.

5. He decreed that any property of orphans should be managed by the orphan's paternal relatives, but that the child him/herself should live with the maternal relatives. The purpose of this law: to prevent relatives on either side from killing the orphan in order to confiscate the property. The maternal relatives would not commit such a crime because they did not control the property, while the paternal relatives would not readily have an opportunity to kill a child not residing with them.

6. He devised penalties for soldiers who fled in battle.

7. Diodorus believes his most ingenious measure to be the one concerning the revision of his law codes. Any citizen could propose a revision, but with this unique condition attached: the proposer had to wear a noose around his neck while the Assembly considered the revision. If the Assembly's action was favorable, the noose would be removed. If not, the proposer would be forthwith hanged.

Diodorus states that on only three occasions did anyone propose revisions to any of Charondas' laws, and that all three times, the revisions were approved.

One of Charondas' own laws proved to be his undoing. He had enacted a measure forbidding citizens to carry weapons into Assembly meetings. But one day when he entered the Assembly, he forgot that he had a dagger strapped to his side. When his political opponents observed him thus armed, they demanded that he answer to his own law. He did so — by killing himself with the very knife that he had failed to check at the Assembly door.

*The innovations of Zaleucas of Italian Locri* (according to Diodorus Siculus)

Charondas' older contemporary Zaleucas was also a noted lawgiver. In the preamble to his legislation, he stated that the first assumption of any orderly society must be that the gods exist, and that citizens should respect and worship the gods.

Zaleucas' major innovation was not so much in the law code itself, as in the punishments. Wrongdoers, or even potential wrongdoers, were to be subjected to various forms of public humiliation, instead of the more usual penalties, such as fines or exile.

*Lycurgan firsts and innovations* (according to Plutarch's biography)

1. Plutarch records that the first and most important change made by Lycurgus was the establishment of a 28-member Spartan Senate (the *gerousia*).

2. He redistributed the land in such a way that all citizens possessed an equal share.
3. He replaced gold and silver currency with "coinage" made of iron.
4. He outlawed all impractical works of art.
5. He decreed that all citizens consume the same kind of food.
6. He established numerous regulations regarding marriage and parenthood; perhaps the most curious of these was his insistence that newlyweds not live together, but only meet at night for intimacy and togetherness.
7. He decreed that boys, at age seven, be taken from their parents and live in military barracks.
8. He encouraged laconic speech.
9. He was the first military leader to organize his cavalry into squadrons of 50 men each.
10. He ordered Spartan citizens to avoid foreign travel; likewise, he discouraged foreigners from entering Spartan territory.

*Pericles innovations* (according to Plutarch's biography)

1. Pericles was the first politician to distribute lands of captured peoples to Athenian citizens.
2. He was the first to issue two-obol grants to citizens to gain them admission to theatrical performances.
3. He instituted payment for jury duty, offering jurors a stipend of two obols per day.
4. He initiated the construction of the Parthenon, and many other notable building projects.
5. He established the custom of including musical contests in the Panathenaic festival.
6. Plutarch alludes to Pericles' high standing among Athenian leaders by assigning to him the "first place"; he thereby surpassed other powerful figures such as Ephialtes, Myronides, Cimon, Tolmides and Thucydides.
7. Pericles almost always appeared aloof and imperturbable in public. The first time that he displayed any emotion occurred at the funeral of his son Paralus, where he cried openly. (This information appears in chapter 36, although Plutarch seems to contradict himself here, as he had stated in chapter 32 that Pericles also wept at Aspasia's trial.)

*Plato's philosophical firsts*

Diogenes Laertius (3.24–25) lists a number of Platonic innovations:

1. Plato was the first to use dialectic to introduce arguments.
2. He was the first to explain analytical problem solving to Leodamas of Thasos.
3. He was the first "who in philosophical discussion employed the terms antipodes, element, dialectic, quality, oblong number, and, among boundaries, the plane superficies; also, divine providence." (tr. Hicks Vol. I [LCL] 299)
4. Plato was the first philosopher to analyze the power of grammar.
5. He was the first to criticize earlier philosophers.

### Pythagoras' firsts

According to Diogenes Laertius (8.10, 12–14, 46–48), the following innovations are to be credited to the philosopher Pythagoras (fl. late sixth century B.C.):

1. He was the first to assert that friends should consider all possessions to be shared property.
2. He discovered the celebrated geometrical principle that the sides of a right triangle squared are equal to the hypotenuse squared.
3. He was reportedly the first man to suggest a meat diet for athletes (who customarily consumed foodstuffs such as figs, cheese and wheat).
4. He was reportedly the first "to declare that the soul, bound now in this creature, now in that, thus goes on a round ordained of necessity." (tr. Hicks Vol. II [LCL] 333)
5. He introduced into Greece a system of weights and measures.
6. He was the first to identify the morning and evening stars as one and the same.
7. He was the first man referred to by the famous phrase *ipse dixit* ("he himself said [it]").
8. He was reputedly the "first to call the heaven the universe and the earth spherical" (tr. Hicks Vol. II [LCL] 365), although some credit Parmenides or Hesiod with these observations.

There was also a noted boxer named Pythagoras, from Samos. He was the first to box *eutechnos*, "scientifically," i.e., apparently, the first to use strategy rather than mere brute force in this physically demanding event. The flamboyant Pythagoras appeared at Olympia with long flowing hair, and attired in a purple robe.

### Solon's administrative innovations

According to Plutarch's *Life of Solon* (especially 15, and 17–24), Solon was noted for the following:

1. His first act was the cancellation of debts, or (according to other

sources) a reduction in the interest on debts. Later, however, Plutarch asserts that Solon's first move was the repeal of Draco's laws.

2. He set the value of a mina at 100 drachmas; its previous value: 73 drachmas.

3. He reputedly founded the Council of the Areopagus, a deliberative body composed of former archons.

4. He established four categories of citizens, based on wealth and property.

5. He established the *boule*, a collective whose primary responsibility was the setting of the assembly's agenda.

6. He decreed that any citizen remaining neutral during a revolution should be disenfranchised.

7. He enacted a measure against the defamation of deceased citizens.

8. He promulgated numerous regulations affecting the behavior of women.

9. He offered cash awards to athletes who won championships at the Olympic games (500 drachmas) or the Isthmian games (100 drachmas).

10. The only commodity which he permitted to be exported from Attica was olive oil.

11. He initiated legislation concerning marriages and wills, and immigration.

### Thales' firsts

According to Diogenes Laertius (1.24 ff.), the philosopher Thales of Miletus was variously credited with the following:

1. Some ancient sources considered Thales to have been the first philosopher to claim that the soul was immortal.

2. He was the first to discern the nature of the sun's course from one solstice to the next.

3. Some authorities asserted that he was "the first to declare the size of the sun to be one seven hundred and twentieth part of the solar circle, and the size of the moon to be the same fraction of the lunar circle." (tr. Hicks [LCL] Vol. I 25)

4. He was the first to call a month's final day the Thirtieth, and also the first (according to some) to debate matters of natural history.

5. He was the first to draw a right triangle within the circumference of a circle (although some sources credit Pythagoras with this mathematical innovation).

6. He was reputedly the first man to note the four seasons, and the first to divide the year into 365 days.

7. He was the creator of the celebrated proverb *gnothi seauton* ("know yourself").

# Roman

*Augustus' firsts* (according to Suetonius, *Life of Augustus*, unless noted otherwise)

1. The first civil war in which he fought was the siege of Mutina conducted against Mark Antony.

2. Augustus created the province of Egypt, and founded a city called Nicopolis, near Actium, the site of his victory over Mark Antony.

3. The first (of only two) foreign war which he personally commanded was carried out against Dalmatia (35–34 B.C.)

4. He added a fourth category of jurors, the so-called *ducenarii* ("200,000 sesterce men," i.e., those whose net worth amounted to that figure. The other three categories: senators, equestrians and the treasury tribunes.) He also reduced the minimum age for a juror from 35 to 30.

5. He proposed numerous social laws and regulations, including measures dealing with marriage, adultery and divorce.

6. He founded 28 new colonies.

7. On documents requiring his official seal, he first used the image of a sphinx. Later he created his own personalized seal, which was also utilized by succeeding emperors.

8. Several Italian cities designated the first day which he visited them to be their *initium anni*, the "beginning of the year."

9. His first wife was Claudia, Mark Antony's stepdaughter. His first (and only) surviving child, Julia, was first married to his cousin Marcellus.

10. His first residence in Rome was located near the Roman forum, in a house formerly owned by the orator Gaius Licinius Calvus.

11. The first (and only) freedman he ever entertained at dinner was Menas, and only because Menas had provided Augustus information about Sextus Pompey's fleet during the war against Pompey in 36–35.

*Julius Caesar's firsts and innovations 45–44 B.C.*

After putting an end to the civil wars of 48–45, Caesar returned to Rome to propose and implement numerous reforms (after first celebrating no fewer than five triumphal processions, the most magnificent of which was the first, the Gallic triumph.)

1. He reformed the calendar, which had traditionally been based on lunar cycles. The result: a 355-day year, with the additional days inserted in February (but sometimes arbitrarily, or not at all). Caesar decreed a 365-day solar year, with a leap year every quadrennium.

2. He created additional praetors, aediles, and quaestors.

3. He changed the method of choosing magistrates; whereas in the past, all office-holders had been elected, under Caesar's new system, the people would select only half, while he would personally appoint the rest.

4. He improved the efficiency of census-taking, and thus was able to reduce the number of welfare recipients from 320,000 to 150,000.

5. He introduced various travel restrictions, including a measure forbidding any citizen between the ages of 20 and 40 to be out of Italy for more than three consecutive years. He also decreed that no senator's son could leave Italy except on official government business.

6. He established employment quotas for livestock owners: a minimum of one-third of their shepherds had to be freeborn citizens.

7. To entice foreign physicians and teachers to live and work in Rome, he offered them immediate grants of Roman citizenship.

8. He discouraged egregious acts of conspicuous consumption by imposing import taxes on foreign goods, by limiting the use of litters for transport, by restricting the wearing of expensive or gaudy clothing (scarlet robes and pearls, for example), and by regulating the serving of exotic foods at dinner parties.

9. He hoped to beautify the city with various new buildings. The first priority: the construction of a temple dedicated to Mars, on a scale more vast than ever before attempted. He had other similar plans and projects in mind, but none came to fruition, because of his untimely assassination. (Suetonius *Life of Julius Caesar* 34–44, with notes by Rolfe Vol. I [LCL]).

*The Seven Kings: firsts* (according to Livy, unless noted otherwise)
Romulus:

1. His first act as king was to fortify the Palatine Hill.

2. He formed the first Roman Senate, which was originally composed of 100 members.

3. He consecrated Rome's first temple, dedicated to Jupiter Feretrius.
4. He was the first to divide the city of Rome into districts, which were called *curiae*; there were 30 of these *curiae*.
5. He called the first month Martius, in honor of his father, Mars. (Ovid *Fasti* 3)

Romulus was also the first to obtain the *opima spolia*, war spoils seized by a Roman general from his counterpart in the enemy's ranks. Only two other such expropriations occurred during republican times: in 436 B.C., by Aulus Cornelius Cossus, and in 224, by Marcus Claudius Marcellus. (Harper's, s.v. *opima spolia*)

Numa Pompilius:
1. He built the Temple of Janus, and established the tradition that the closing of its gates signified that Rome was at peace.
2. He devised a 12-month lunar calendar, and he was the first Roman leader to designate certain days when business could and could not be conducted.
3. He was responsible for many innovations in religious matters, especially in the creation of priestly offices and in the systematized observance of religious ceremonies.

Tullus Hostilius:
1. He annexed the Caelian Hill to Rome, and ordered the construction of an enlarged Senate house, the Curia Hostilia, which retained that name even to Livy's time.

Ancus Martius:
1. The Aventine Hill was peopled for the first time, by captives taken from Rome's attack on the nearby town of Politorium.
2. He added the Janiculum Hill to the city's territory. The first bridge over the Tiber, the Pons Sublicius, was built to connect the Janiculum with the rest of Rome.
3. The Carcer (city jail) was established during his kingship.

Lucius Tarquinius Priscus:
1. He was the first to "campaign" for the kingship, by soliciting support from the plebeians. He was also the first to deliver campaign-style speeches.
2. He doubled the size of the Roman Senate, from 100 to 200 members.
3. The site for the Circus Maximus was determined and measured. Bleacher seats were constructed, and regular games (the Ludi

Romani) were instituted. He also initiated construction of the great Capitoline temple to Jupiter Optimus Maximus.

Servius Tullius:
1. He originated the census, which divided the citizenry into classifications (centuries) according to their wealth, primarily to determine the extent of armor and weaponry each man had to supply in wartime.
2. He annexed two more hills, the Quirinal and the Viminal.

Lucius Tarquinius Superbus:
1. He was the first to ignore the tradition that the king ought to consult with the Senate on matters of statecraft. Instead, he chose to rule more as a dictator, soliciting advice only from a small circle of family members.
2. Turnus Herdonius, a Latin noble and an opponent of Tarquinius Superbus, was the first to suffer a particularly gruesome method of execution: he was confined in a wooden crate weighed down by rocks, and hurled into a river.
3. The first sewer, the Cloaca Maxima, was constructed during Tarquinius' reign.

# Bibliography

Astius, D. F. *Lexicon Platonicum, sive Vocum Platonicarum Index*. New York, (reprinted) 1969.

Balsdon, J. P. V. D. *Life and Leisure in Ancient Rome*. New York, 1969.

Betant, E.-A. *Lexicon Thucydideum*. Hildesheim, 1961.

Birch, Cordelia Margaret. *Concordantia et Index Caesaris — Concordance and Index to Caesar*. Hildesheim, 1989.

Boissevain, U. P. *Cassii Dionis Cocceiani: Historiarum Romanarum Quae Supersunt*. Frankfurt, 1969.

Bonnellus, E. *Lexicon Quintilianeum*. Hildesheim, 1962.

Boren, Henry C. *Roman Society* (2nd edition). Lexington (MA), 1992.

Briggs, Ward W., Jr. *Concordantia in Varronis Libros De Re Rustica*. Hildesheim, 1983.

Broughton, T. Robert S. *The Magistrates of the Roman Republic*. New York, 1951, 1952.

Butler, H.E. (tr.). *The Institutio Oratoria of Quintilian* (LCL). Cambridge (MA), 1920.

Campbell, Malcolm. *Index Verborum in Apollonium Rhodium*. Hildesheim, 1983.

Caplan, Harry (tr.). *[Cicero] Ad C. Herennium* (LCL). Cambridge (MA), 1954.

Cowell, Frank R. *Cicero and the Roman Republic*. Baltimore, 1962.

De Camp, L. Sprague. *The Ancient Engineers*. New York, 1963.

Deferrari, Roy J., Sr. M. Inviolata Barry, Martin R. P. McGuire. *A Concordance of Ovid*. Washington DC, 1939.

Dunbar, Henry (revised by Benedetto Marzullo). *A Complete Concordance to the Odyssey of Homer*. Darmstadt, 1962.

Evelyn-White, Hugh G. (tr.). *Ausonius* (LCL). Cambridge (MA), 1919.

_____. Hesiod: *Theogony* [etc.] (LCL). Cambridge (MA), 1914.

Fairclough, H. Rushton (tr.). *Horace: Satires* [etc.] (LCL). Cambridge (MA), 1926.

Falconer, William Armistead (tr.). *Cicero: De Divinatione* [etc.] (LCL). Cambridge (MA), 1923.

Famerie, Etienne. *Concordantia in Appianum: Concordance d'Appien.* Hildesheim, 1993.

Feder, Lillian. *Apollo Handbook of Classical Literature.* New York, 1964.

Foster, B. O. (tr.). *Livy* (Vol. IV, LCL). Cambridge (MA), 1926.

Fowler, Harold North (tr.). *Plutarch's Moralia* (Vol. V, LCL). Cambridge (MA), 1936.

Freese, John Henry (tr.). *Cicero: Pro Quinctio* [etc.] (LCL). Cambridge (MA), 1930.

Fyfe, W. Hamilton (tr.). *Aristotle: The Poetics* (LCL). Cambridge (MA), 1927.

Granger, Frank (tr.). *Vitruvius on Architecture* (LCL). Cambridge (MA), 1931.

Grant, Michael. *Myths of the Greeks and Romans.* New York, 1962.

Graves, Robert. *The Greek Myths.* Baltimore, 1955.

Gulick, Charles Burton (tr.). *Athenaeus: The Deipnosophists* (LCL). Cambridge (MA), 1927.

Hadas, Moses. *A History of Greek Literature.* New York, 1950.

*Harper's Dictionary of Classical Literature and Antiquities.* New York, 1896.

Hendrickson, G. L. (tr.). *Cicero: Brutus* (LCL). Cambridge (MA), 1939.

Hicks, R. D. (tr.). *Diogenes Laertius* (LCL). Cambridge (MA), 1935.

Howard, A. A.; C. N. Jackson. *Index Verborum C. Suetoni Tranquilli.* Cambridge (MA), 1922.

Hubbell, H. M. (tr.). *Cicero: Orator* (LCL). Cambridge (MA), 1939.

Jones, W. H. S. (tr.). *Pliny: Natural History* (Vols. VI–X, LCL). Cambridge (MA), 1951.

Kelling, Lucile, Albert Suskin. *Index Verborum Iuvenalis.* Chapel Hill (NC), 1951.

Ker, Walter (tr.). *Martial: Epigrams* (LCL). Cambridge (MA), 1919.

Lesky, Albin. *A History of Greek Literature* (tr. by James Willis and Cornelis de Heer). New York, 1966.

MacDonald, C. (tr.). *Cicero: In Catilinam I–IV* [etc.] (LCL). Cambridge (MA), 1976.

McDougall, J. Iain. *Lexicon in Diodorum Siculum.* Hildesheim, 1983.

Morford, Mark P. O., Robert J. Lenardon. *Classical Mythology.* New York, 1971.

Nixon, Paul (tr.). *Plautus* (LCL). Cambridge (MA), 1916.

Oldfather, C. H. (tr.). *Diodorus of Sicily* (Vols. I–VI, LCL). Cambridge (MA), 1933.

Oldfather, W. A., H. V. Canter, K. M. Abbott. *Index Verborum Ciceronis Epistularum.* Hildesheim, 1965.

*Oxford Classical Dictionary* (3rd edition; edited by Simon Hornblower; Antony Spawforth). New York, 1996.

*Oxford History of the Classical World* (edited by John Boardman; Jasper Griffin; Oswyn Murray). New York, 1986.

Perrin, Bernadotte (tr.). *Plutarch's Lives: Pericles* [etc.] (LCL). Cambridge (MA), 1916.

Powell, J. Enoch. *A Lexicon to Herodotus.* Hildesheim, 1960.

Prendergast, Guy Lushington (revised by Benedetto Marzullo). *A Complete Concordance to the Iliad of Homer.* Darmstadt, 1962.

Rackham, H. (tr.). *Aristotle: The Athenian Constitution* [etc.] (LCL). Cambridge (MA), 1935.

_____ (tr.). *Pliny: Natural History* (Vols. I–V, LCL). Cambridge (MA), 1938.

Ramsay, G. G. (tr.). *Juvenal and Persius* (LCL). Cambridge (MA), 1918.

Rolfe, J. C. (tr.). *Sallust* (LCL). Cambridge (MA), 1921.

_____ (tr.). *Suetonius* (LCL). Cambridge (MA), 1913.

Rose, H. J. *A Handbook of Greek Literature.* New York, 1934.

Rumpel, Ioannes. *Lexicon Pindaricum.* Hildesheim, 1961.

Sandys, John Edwin. *A Short History of Classical Scholarship.* Cambridge (MA), 1915.

_____ (tr.). *Pindar* (LCL). Cambridge (MA), 1915.

Schlesinger, Alfred C. (tr.). *Livy* (Vol. XIV, LCL). Cambridge (MA), 1959.

Scott-Kilvert, Ian (tr.). *The Rise and Fall of Athens: Nine Greek Lives by Plutarch.* New York, 1960.

Shipley, Frederick W. (tr.). *Velleius Paterculus: Compendium of Roman History* (LCL). Cambridge (MA), 1924.

Siedschlag, Edgar. *Martial-Konkordanz.* Hildesheim, 1979.

Smith, Charles (tr.). *Thucydides* (LCL). London, New York, 1923.

Sturz, F. G. *Lexicon Xenophonteum*. Hildesheim, 1964.

Tebben, Joseph R. *Hesiod-Konkordanz: A Computer Concordance to Hesiod*. Hildesheim, 1977.

Warmington, E. H. (tr.). *Remains of Old Latin* (Vol. I, LCL). Cambridge (MA), 1935.

Warwick, Henrietta Holm. *A Vergil Concordance*. Minneapolis, 1975.

White, Horace (tr.). *Appian's Roman History* (LCL). Cambridge (MA), 1912.

Williams, W. Glynn (tr.). *Cicero: The Letters to His Friends* (LCL). Cambridge (MA), 1927.

Wyttenbach, Daniel. *Lexicon Plutarcheum*. Hildesheim, 1962.

Zimmerman, J. E. *Dictionary of Classical Mythology*. New York, 1964.

# Index of Entries

**Category Two:**
**Firsts in Politics, Oratory,**
**Law, Government** 27–52

## Category Three: Firsts in Military and Foreign Affairs 53–66

**Category Four:
Firsts in Art, Architecture,
Literature, Science**  67–100

Two supremely alliterative lines of
poetry 97
Vergil's first poem 97
First speakers in dialogues, plays and
poems 97–100

## Category Five:
## Miscellaneous Firsts 101–125

Augustus' first residence in Rome 108
Augustus' first task 108
best time to set sail 101
Death to the first Athenian 101
dole's pecking order 108
Elephantine firsts 108
Farming firsts 108–109
first altar dedicated to Augustus at
Lugdunum 109
first and only instance of lightning
striking twice 101
first — and only — man to speak 22
languages [Mithridates VI] 109
first appearance of Galeria Copiola 109
first artificial gold and silver foliage 109
first aviary 109
first benefactor in the *alimenta* system
[Titus Julius Helvia] 109
first blessing for a sailor 101
first brigand encountered by Theseus
[Periphetes] 101–102
first brother to see birds 109
first bullfight 109
first capture of Troy 102
first celebration of a *lectisternium* 110
first celebration of the Floralia 110
first celebration of the Ludi Sullanae
Victoriae 110
first city in Italy [Lanuvium] 110
first civilian use of the title *princeps
juventutis* 110
first cloak-clad emperor to preside at
gladiatorial games [Claudius] 110
first craftsmen's wares 110–111
first crown 102
first cultivated roses 102
first Cynic [Antisthenes of Athens] 102
first day of the Roman month 111
first days of each season 111
first day's torture 111
first dinner item 111

first *Dives* ("Rich") 111
first division of agriculture 111
first domesticated animals 112
first Dorian community 102
first Egyptian to use a divine Greek
title 102
first elaborate dining room furniture
112
first emperor to devalue Roman coinage
[Nero] 112
first endeavor for a young man 102
first farm-bred livestock 112
first food of Latium 112
A first for the new emperor Claudius
112
first force for decency 112
first formal gardens 112
first free banquet at a gladiatorial show
113
first game farm 113
first hour of the Roman day 113
first indication of Bacchic rites in Italy
113
first item in a petitionary prayer 113
first king of Troy [Teucer] 113
first land allotments 113
first letter as an omen 113
first Ludi Apollinares 113
first man to enter seven chariots at the
Olympic games [Alcibiades] 102–103
first Maximus 114
first meal of the day 114
first meat diets for Olympic athletes
103
first moon and the last moon 114
first multiple exhibition of lions 114
first naked Olympic athlete [Orsippus]
103
first name of Baiae 114
first name of Beneventum 114
first name of the Black Sea 103
first notable Octavius 114
first noted wine vintage 115
first of the Ptolemaic rulers to learn
Egyptian [Cleopatra VII] 115
first of the Seven Sages 103
first Olympic winners 103–104
first palm awarded to victorious athletes
104
first people 104

# Index of Names

4/00